THE STORY OF ARCHIE THE TALKING SNOWMAN

THE STORY OF ARCHIE THE TALKING SNOWMAN

& Akron's History of Christmas Attractions

by Joanna Wilson

1701 Press
Akron, Ohio

Proudly published by 1701 Press, Akron, Ohio

Printed and bound in the United States of America
First Printing 2015

ISBN 978-0-9842699-7-6 (pbk)

Cover illustration figures created by
Samantha Tailor Hudson • snow. • www.snowfosho.com

Design: Dominic Caruso
http://domcaruso.com

OTHER BOOKS BY JOANNA WILSON

The Christmas TV Companion: a Guide to Cult Classics, Strange Specials, & Outrageous Oddities

Tis the Season TV: the Encyclopedia of Christmas-Themed Episodes, Specials, and Made-for-TV Movies

Merry Musical Christmas, Volume One: The Best Christmas Music in Television Sitcoms & Dramas

A is for Akron: an A to Z list of Akron's Places and things that make us Smile (with Karen Starr)

IF YOUR CHILDHOOD CHRISTMAS MEMORIES INCLUDE VISITING A TWENTY-FOOT-TALL TALKING SNOWMAN WITH FLASHING RED EYES, THEN YOU UNDOUBTEDLY GREW UP IN AKRON, OHIO.

THE STORY OF ARCHIE THE SNOWMAN IS THE STORY OF THE PEOPLE WHO HELPED MAKE ARCHIE MORE THAN JUST A STORE CHRISTMAS ATTRACTION.

IT'S ALSO THE SURPRISING STORY OF AKRON'S HUNDRED-YEAR HISTORY OF ELEGANT, EXTRAVAGANT, AND OCCASIONALLY PLAIN WEIRD RETAIL CHRISTMAS ATTRACTIONS—FROM THE ENCHANTING DOWNTOWN WINDOWS OF O'NEIL'S & POLSKY'S, TO TALKING CHRISTMAS TREES, TRAINED ANIMAL ACTS, & SANTA ARRIVING BY SATELLITE. IT'S THE FASCINATING CONTEXT FOR HOW & WHY ARCHIE CAME TO BE.

TABLE OF CONTENTS

i	Introduction
1	Prologue: The Story of Archie
7	The Making of the 'Man: The History of Archie
35	Retailing Rivals
39	Frosted Windowpanes: Downtown Window Displays
40	*Shop Early!*
48	*Locally Made Toys*
64	*The Singing Tower*
79	Sacred Window Displays of O'Neil's and Polsky's
83	How Santa Came To Town
84	*DeWitt Motors' Alaskan Santa*
95	*Downtown Parades*
99	Now Appearing: Santa's Celebrity Guests
109	Christmas Monkey Business: Organ Grinders
113	Winter Wonderlands: Store Walk-Throughs & In-Store Attractions
127	*The Tree of Lights*
139	Yuletide Yakkers: Talking Attractions Before & After Archie
147	Christmas Comics
153	Splendor on a String: the Puppet Shows
163	Free Childcare, While You Shop!
167	Archie Returns: a Social Networking Success Story

ACKNOWLEDGEMENTS

The author wishes to express her thanks to the members of the community whose help, support, and encouragement have helped to make this book possible.

I wish to offer special thanks to Tommy Uplinger and Ra'ul Umaña for sitting through many interviews with me, patiently answering my questions, and sharing their passion for Archie.

I greatly appreciate the help and assistance of Lawrence and Cynthia Nixon, Jeanne Jordan, Brenda Fargo, and the fine people at Cornerstone Church at Portage Lakes for providing me information about the current status of the downtown display items. I wish to thank Lauren VonVesterfield, Jason Pullin, and Marianna Alacchi for their time in helping me understand the efforts that went into installing Archie at Lock 3 in 2012. Additional assistance from David Lieberth, Tish Jernigan, and Michael Cohill are also appreciated.

The many months I spent researching and reading the newspapers on the microfilm machines in the Special Collections of the Akron-Summit County Public Library were made more pleasant and fruitful by the kindness and assistance of Judy James and the entire staff of the department. My long days spent in front of the machines were also made brighter by the friendliness of two library security guards, Brandon Brown and Ron Goodman. Thanks for your smiles and daily greetings, guys!

I'm also grateful for additional help and assistance from

Ghoulardi aficionado Don "Kaptin Ignatz" Clark, the archivist Sister Elizabeth Wood at Sisters of Notre Dame of Chardon Province, the Barberton Historical Society, Sarah Hays, local history librarian at the Barberton Public Library, Jennifer Van Volkinburg at McKinley Inc., and Kate Miller at Simon Property Group.

I also wish to thank all the people who stepped forward to share information and their memories of Archie the Talking Snowman: D.X. Ferris, Erick Bognar, Scott Robishaw, Bob Ignizio, Jill Grimm, Ronda Roxbury, Mickey MacAdam, Alex Dorko, Greg Berg, MaryLou Fogle, Heather Quinn, Terrie Moeller, Kristen, Leslie Martin Matheny, Candie Ujhazy, Amanda Knight, Jammin' Paul Hively, and David A. Burkett's parents—David Burkett and Karen Carver.

In memory of Ra'ul Umaña who helped build, maintain, and give voice to Archie, and who gave Archie his heart.

And in memory of David A. Burkett who helped bring Archie back to us.

This book wouldn't have been possible without their help.

INTRODUCTION

Tom the Talking Horse? A nine foot-tall Raggedy Ann doll? A walk-through zeppelin "ride" to the North Pole? A Santa that arrives by helicopter to Polsky's downtown parking deck? For nearly a century, young Akronites have witnessed these fantastic magical Christmas experiences. A giant talking snowman named Archie doesn't seem that far fetched or even out of the ordinary. Yet he is.

Akron was an extremely competitive marketplace at Christmas each year as downtown stores, and eventually plazas and suburban malls joined the contest. The unique competition over the attention of Akron's shoppers benefited us all with an ever escalating build up of Christmas enchantment and entertainment. During our city's long history, luxury shopping in the downtown city center rivaled that in other large cities including Chicago, Baltimore, St. Louis and Denver. The shopping was at a level with larger cities, and the windows were extremely good too. Although New York City has been considered—deservedly so—the source of the highest quality in Christmas window displays, I've found that Akron also created incredibly extravagant window displays and utilized nationally known window display designs that were available in New York and throughout the country, including markets much larger than ours. Many people in Akron still remember the fantasy and magic of O'Neil's and Polsky's Christmas window displays.

Akron's retailers didn't just create awe-inspiring Christmas window displays, the competition for shoppers' attention also included in-store attractions with fanciful Santa Land walk-through experiences, live clowns, organ grinders, and TV celebrity appearances. Holiday parades with giant balloons marched down Main Street, puppet shows by nationally touring troupes entertained the crowds, and Santa Claus' arrival at downtown stores became a special event worthy of front page coverage in the local newspaper.

Until it was gone. As the Rubber City flourished, so did the competition over residents' Christmas shopping money. When our economy changed, and consumer habits changed, so did the draw and eventually the need for Christmas attractions. The history of Akron-area Christmas attractions and Archie is actually a reflection of the changing consumer habits associated with Christmas shopping and retailing in general. In this story, you'll find that it's not over-commercialism, consumerism, or the lack of holiday spirit that changed Christmas traditions—but rather *how* we consume. How we consume and buy in Akron, and America, has everything to do with the history of our Christmas traditions and Archie the Snowman.

But as I see it, this story about Akron's history of Christmas attractions has a happy ending. As we march into the twenty-first century coming to terms with what it means to no longer be the rubber capital of the world, on the cusp of an entirely new identity, and what kind of shopping can be done downtown, we are bolstered by a meaningful history of traditions. Not only that, we also have some traditions still available to us—even if some of us don't realize it.

Researching Archie's origins, I came across a long, rich past of Christmas attractions in this city. Archie was just one of many attractions meant to promote a store and lure visitors to shop there. Amongst the decades of mechanical window displays, in-store Santa Land walk-throughs, opportunities to sit on Santa's lap, celebrity appearances, and puppet shows, Archie the Snowman became a local holiday institution.

In the early 1970s, I was one of the thousands of children brought to Chapel Hill Mall to talk with Archie. However, the mysterious voice from nowhere and the flashing red eyes scared me. I never did step up to the platform to speak with Archie, but I never forgot him either. When I went to college out of town, I remember talking about the unforgettable twenty-foot-tall mall snowman from my hometown. And after the internet was readily available in the 1990s, Archie the Talking Snowman was one of the first image searches I ever typed on a computer to verify my childhood memories. Later, I was one of the thousands of people who joined the Bring Archie Back to Chapel Hill Mall Facebook group. I followed the story of Tommy Uplinger and David Burkett who worked to bring Archie to Lock 3. And, I wrote about Archie's debut at Lock 3 in November 2012 for my website *Akron Empire*. Knowing how important Archie the Snowman is to Akron residents, I made sure to include a photo of Archie in the local history/ nostalgia book *A is for Akron*. The more I thought about it, the more I knew the story of Archie was a compelling tale.

I limited myself when researching Archie and Akron's history of Christmas attractions to the experiences created by retailers and retail centers such as plazas and malls. Archie was created in the context of that competitive selling environment. However, Akron's rich history includes many other Christmas memories, including private ceremonies, church group parties, children's charity drives, fraternal group holiday celebrations, decades worth of extravagant lighting and decorated homes, theater performances, etc. The long and lavish history of these Akron experiences can be documented by someone else who can do them justice. I had to forgo research and discussion of the traditions of ballet performances of *The Nutcracker,* music concerts, Stan Hywet holiday events, First Night New Year's Eve events, extravagant rubber company parties for employees, and the like to concentrate on retail attractions.

My research also revealed that national company stores and chains largely ignored annual Christmas attractions and the competition with local stores in downtown Akron. While national chain stores such as Sears, Woolworth's, Montgomery

Ward, Kresge's, Kmart, and JC Penney's offered Christmas sales discounts, beautiful store decorations, and sometimes even in-store Santa Clauses to visit, these retailers did little to compete with the local stores' extravagant window displays, walk-through experiences, and escalation in Christmas attractions. By focusing on the local retail Christmas attractions, we can see the context and culture which created the splendor that dominated downtown Akron throughout the twentieth century—and inspired the likes of Archie the Talking Snowman.

For those that didn't grow up visiting Archie the Talking Snowman or those who weren't raised in Akron, I think you'll discover the history of Akron's Christmas attractions a satisfying experience. You'll also come to better understand why thousands of our city's residents are crazy for Archie—Akron's holiday celebrity.

My research into the history of Archie led me on an unexpected journey. No one I interviewed about their role in working with Archie at the mall ever expected to be explaining themselves after forty years. It became clear early in the research and interviews that few people's memories would ever match anyone's timelines of events as well. That's understandable. I began looking into old newspapers for stories and articles about Archie—most of which contradicted each other. Surprisingly, I stumbled across a long legacy of advertisements describing—often in detail—exactly what was to be seen and experienced at the downtown stores, plazas, and malls. I also reasoned that these retailers were paying a lot of money for these ads, therefore their accuracy would be far greater than personal recollections. Archives from the actual retailers are nonexistent. O'Neil's and Polsky's closed shop several decades ago. Rolling Acres is abandoned, and Chapel Hill and Summit Mall have each changed ownership several times. There is no archive that I know of saved by these companies to document their past. And who can blame them? Annual Christmas attractions and promotions were meant to be short-term efforts to make money—not document a city's cultural history.

But as you read the book, you'll see how much information

can actually be found within advertisements. To be fair, I also pulled information from news stories, editorials, Around Town features, as well as personal accounts of cherished memories. Nothing would please me more than this book's presence inspiring someone to dig out of a forgotten closet more information about our own Christmas cultural heritage. I also consulted several books for additional research, the best of which include *The History of the Snowman* (2007) by Bob Eckstein, *Holidays on Display* (2007) by William L. Bird, Jr., and *Through the Shopping Glass: A Century of New York Christmas Windows* (2000) by Sheryll Bellman.

Archie may have been a lure by the mall to bring shoppers in, but don't under-estimate the powerful nostalgia associated with promotional characters. The character Rudolph the Red-Nosed Reindeer was created as a promotional tool by Montgomery Ward to promote their store. A song, a theatrical release cartoon, and 1964 stop motion animated TV special later, and Rudolph is still one of the most popular and beloved Christmas icons. Archie has power too—he's inspired tens of thousands of residents to visit him each year.

The story of our Christmas attractions is an Akron story—one that couldn't have existed anywhere but here and reflects our unique identity. Archie the Talking Snowman is not just a holiday tradition but a piece of Akron history. Akron is a city that has been forced to endure great changes. Many people didn't like all the changes and they worked to bring back a little piece of happiness to share with their children and grandchildren. Akronites are used to repurposing their spaces and moving into the future. I like that Archie can be counted among those sentimental success stories.

Has your grandmother ever shared with you her experiences of walking through a submarine attraction at O'Neil's in order to sit on Santa's lap? Are you old enough to remember that Goodyear made parade balloons for the Macy's Thanksgiving Day parade in New York City, and that most likely some of the same balloons were also used in holiday parades right down our own Main Street? Did you know that Christmas store windows downtown on several occasions were filled with Disney movie mechanical figures which corresponded to rubber Disney toys manufactured locally? Did you know that Archie is *not* the first talking Christmas attraction in Akron—and he's not even the weirdest? Were you aware that a social networking campaign to bring back Archie the Snowman became a national media phenomenon, inspiring the city to re-create our own meaningful Christmas tradition? Although online shopping may have forever changed how we shop, it was also online social media that helped return a cherished Christmas tradition. Let me tell you all about the story of Archie.

THE STORY OF ARCHIE

Hundreds of people gathered inside Chapel Hill Mall on the morning of Saturday, November 22nd, 2014. It was the unveiling of Akron's own Archie the Talking Snowman—an annual event that is typically filled with anticipation for children. But this year's debut of Archie was different. Although children have nervously waited for Archie's opening each year, in 2014 the adults in the gathering crowd were the ones with the most excitement in their eyes. The giant talking snowman was finally returning to the place where he made his start forty-six years earlier. Chapel Hill Mall was Archie's home and nothing is more heart-warming than a return home for Christmas.

Archie the Snowman looked much like he always did. He was still a three-tiered snowman that stood as tall as the ceiling. Archie also continued to wear a hat, scarf, mittens, vertical buttons down his front, and a big smile on his face. One discernible difference in appearance was his most striking feature—his eyes. When Archie last stood in the mall, during the 2003 holiday season, he had red eyes that flashed when he spoke. Now Archie sported cooler, more friendly, blue eyes that were easier to stare up at. It is Archie's eyes that most adults who experienced Chapel Hill's talking Christmas attraction when they were young still talk about. The stuff of dreams.

On that morning in November, a line of adults and children formed and wrapped around Archie and the surrounding Archie

Land display. The mall anticipated the crowds and placed velvet ropes and barriers up to help people form an orderly queue. Young parents in their twenties, older parents and even grandparents stood in line with babies, toddlers, and school-aged children. Many were standing in line with several children. And as the line grew longer and longer, the excitement in the center of the mall grew and grew. Everyone had one question on their minds: When would Archie begin addressing his faithful believers?

Crowds of people also gathered just beyond those waiting in line. These were mostly adults, witnesses looking to participate in Archie's return—even if they weren't going to individually speak with him. Among them was Ra'ul Umaña, the former Chapel Hill employee who not only worked as the voice of Archie for many years but also as a seasonal employee at the mall, helping to install Archie and the elaborate Archie Land year after year. Umaña, now dying of cancer, came to the 2014 kick-off event accompanied by his family to see Archie's return and his labor of love. Dressed as Father Christmas, Ra'ul's enthusiasm was not overlooked, despite his frail health. Also in the crowd was Tommy Uplinger, with his wife and young son Liam. Uplinger started the social networking movement in 2011 that helped make Archie's return a reality. Painfully absent on this day was Tommy's friend, David Burkett, who assisted in rallying public support and attention on behalf of bringing back Archie. Burkett had died suddenly and unexpectedly in March of 2014 and his absence was felt by many in the crowd that day. The community of people who organized to restore Akron's favorite Christmas tradition were also in the crowd at Chapel Hill that day. Strangers who had become friends during the months and years of efforts to rebuild Archie for Akron's children were there to see their work come to fruition.

Archie's much anticipated return to Chapel Hill also meant that the mall staff had to conceal the twenty-foot-tall frozen figure from the public while he was being installed during the weeks before the November 22nd event. Giant curtains were hung around the presentation space to hide Archie and the Archie Land display that sprawled across the mall floor. As testament to people's anticipation

Archie the Snowman at Chapel Hill Mall, 2014. Photo: Dominic Caruso

and eagerness, mobile phone photos of the curtained area began popping up on social media sites in the weeks before the kick-off event. Akronites were excited to see what lay behind the closed curtains. Mind you, these weren't children posting photos—these were adults—eager fans nonetheless who wanted to snatch a glimpse of what can only be seen once a year.

The large holiday kick-off event at the mall included all sorts of Archie the Snowman promotions, including Archie buttons, t-shirts, paper elf hats, and other various prizes and giveaways. The local newspaper, *The Akron Beacon Journal,* sent a reporter and a photographer to cover the event and the story landed on the cover of the Sunday paper's Community section.

It was an exciting day in Akron because it had been eleven years since Archie had been at the mall. Some in the crowd at the mall knew that Archie had been spending the holiday season of the past two years in downtown's Lock 3, while others only knew that Archie had been retired at Chapel Hill after the Christmas season in 2003. Adults who grew up visiting Archie brought their children to experience a bit of the thrill of sharing a conversation with a twenty-foot-tall Akron Christmas tradition. But the children in line at the mall on that day mostly didn't know about the tradition, nor did they care. On that day, Akron's youngest only cared about what Archie was going to do today. As it should be. Saturday, November 22nd was only one day, the first day, of Archie's long reign as the center of attention. He would continue to talk with children and offer warm holiday greetings to thousands more at Chapel Hill through the end of the 2014 holiday season.

When the magical snowman finally did address the crowd, after a brief greeting to everyone gathered around, Archie asked to first speak with Tommy Uplinger and his six-year-old son, Liam. It was a touching and inspiring moment to witness the man who had worked so hard to bring Archie back to Akron share the moment with his young son. Quickly it was someone else's turn to step up to the microphone and chat with everyone's frozen friend. The morning's kick-off event turned into a long afternoon and evening as Archie continued talking to visitors until the close of business. And this was just the start of the six week holiday season.

Archie's return to Chapel Hill Mall had been a long trip. It had been a twisty, difficult journey for a Christmas attraction meant to entice shoppers to a local mall during the holidays. It's not just a long, complicated story—it's an interesting one too. A story about Akron history.

THE MAKING OF THE 'MAN:
THE HISTORY OF ARCHIE

The origin of Archie the Snowman is a humble story, to be sure. Chapel Hill Mall on the city's northeast side, where North Akron meets Cuyahoga Falls and Tallmadge, opened during the start of the holiday season in 1966. There was tremendous promise and excitement in that first year—Chapel Hill was only the second indoor shopping mall in Akron. The first was Summit Mall which began business one year earlier, in 1965, but it was located on the opposite side of town, in Fairlawn, in the city's northwest corner. For decades, Akronites did their Christmas shopping downtown and the department stores O'Neil's and Polsky's had gone to great lengths each year with their fantasy window displays and elaborate Santa Land walk-through experiences to entice and entertain the shoppers. However, shopping malls offered free and ample parking in neighborhoods closer to suburbanites who had chosen to move further away from the city's center. Malls also wanted to lure holiday shoppers with their own eye-catching Christmas attractions, and Archie the Talking Snowman was added to Chapel Hill's inclusion of Santa Claus for their seasonal program.

When Archie the Snowman came into existence, he seemed to be an entirely new and novel creation. In fact, Akron has a long rich history of retail Christmas attractions—and to be frank, Archie is just one on a long list of interactive, talking creatures. 1968 saw the introduction of the two-story-tall, talking snowman. Was a talking snowman really unique enough to hold the attention and imaginations of Akron's youngest and their parents? You'd better believe it—Archie was an immediate success and would return to the mall each holiday season for more than three decades, outlasting all the other talking Christmas attractions in our city. The magic that swirled around Archie made Chapel Hill Mall the destination for family shopping for years. Not only that but other merchants sought to imitate Archie's charm and spectacle for their holiday attractions in order to keep up with the growing demand for entertainment and holiday shoppers' money in years to come.

There's no denying that Archie has created warm and meaningful Christmas memories for generations of Akron residents. Archie has connected young minds to enchanting fantasies that inspire and provide an outlet for adults to nurture the happy child inside each one of us. But we shouldn't dismiss or put out of our minds the true purpose of Archie's existence. Archie was created not just to entertain, help create Christmas memories, and inspire the Christmas spirit—but to promote the mall and bring shoppers through the doors. To put it more bluntly, malls need customers for the holiday shopping season, the biggest shopping season of the year, and having a draw like a giant, talking snowman is an alluring attraction. I certainly don't mean to be so crass and cynical as to suggest that Archie's sole purpose has been for commercial reasons, but the cost and effort required to create and maintain such an attraction doesn't come from simple altruism.

Before you lose your Christmas spirit, let's keep this in perspective: Akron's much-romanticized, decades-long tradition of Christmas window displays filled with storybook characters were also hosted by merchants, most notably downtown at O'Neil's and Polsky's. Those glorious, magical windows and the stores' festive decorations were also created to entice shoppers to be loyal and to spend their hard earned money inside the store. Yet most people would agree that our community has benefitted and has been culturally enriched from the retailers' elaborate and nostalgic holiday promotions despite their commercial setting.

Visiting a department store Santa Claus is a retail Christmas attraction intended to entertain, and—yes—bring potential

Visit the Talking Snow Man

ф

at Chapel Hill's

Snow Village:
(center court)

**Bring the children!
Our snow man will
talk to them
daily between
4 and 8:30 o'clock.**

Visit every store in the Chapel Hill Shopping Community
Enjoy the comfort of Chapel Hill's covered, completely
air-conditioned Mall for your Christmas shopping.

A&P	Gray Drug Store	New York Bakery	Singer Sewing
Akron National Bank	Holiday Shoes	Nabil Shoes	Spencer Gifts
Andre Duval Beauty Salon	Household Finance	O'Neil's	Stefani's
Baker's Shoes	Koch's	Parklane Hosiers	Tuff Styles
Barricini's	Kroger's	Paul Harris	Thom McAn Shoes
Clarkins Optical	Lang's	Penneys	Tie Rak
Cleveland Fabrics	Le Petit Cafe	Petrie's	The Village Store
Cowell & Hubbard	Memory Lane	Pollyanna	Walden's Book Store
Chapel Hill Barber Shop	Metzger's	Record Land	Winkleman's
Cinema I & II	Miller's Jr. Shoe Part	Richman Brothers	Woolworth's
Dixie Hats	Mode O'Day	Rossi Toys	Yale's
Fuflik Shoes	National Shirt Shop	Sears	
Fanny Farmer Candies			
Flagg Brothers Shoes	ON BUCHHOLZER BLVD Goodyear Service Store, Goodyear Bank		
Evrwood Outmfts	ON INDEPENDENCE AVE Forest City Interals		

CHAPEL HILL
IS A
CHRISTMAS
WONDERLAND

November 17, 1968 newspaper ad for "The Talking Snowman" at Chapel Hill Mall.

shoppers into the building. If this revelation threatens your conception of Christmas, you should know that Santa Claus has been a popular holiday retail tradition for more than one hundred years and civilization hasn't collapsed in on itself yet. Chapel Hill Mall welcomed shoppers to sit with their first Santa Claus in the mall's center court in 1967—just one year after opening. In fact, the mall created a tremendous to-do about welcoming Santa to the mall in that first year. Jolly Ol' St. Nick arrived riding atop a live elephant.

At that time, the owners of Chapel Hill knew what all other local retailers knew. Santa Claus is a must-have fixture for kiddies to visit at your establishment during Christmas. However, every major retailer in town offered the same opportunity. In 1967 in Akron, children could visit Santa Claus and tell him their Christmas wishes at Chapel Hill Mall, Summit Mall, at Polsky's and O'Neil's downtown, as well as Arlington Plaza, Lakemore Plaza, Akron Square Shopping Center, Coventry Plaza, Stow-Kent Plaza, State Road Shopping Center, and more. Parents could even take their little ones to any one of eight Lujan's Burger Boy Restaurants to sit on Santa's lap. In 1967, Akron was infested with men in red suits.

That's what makes Archie's creation necessary and such an act of genius. How does a mall's owner compete for attention in a marketplace saturated with Christmas attractions? He doesn't replace the much beloved Santa Claus—he adds another attraction. An attraction so wondrous and breathtaking everyone must come to see it for themselves. A cheerful snowman that is so large he touches the ceiling makes for great advertising—an eye-catching seasonal image that's familiar but different than Santa, capable of filling newspaper ads and inspiring awe. In 1968, Chapel Hill Mall's owner and developer Richard Buchholzer introduced this holiday attraction, Archie the Snowman, and started a Christmas tradition that is still close to the hearts of many.

Snowmen have long been used as commercial characters in advertising and entertainment. Plump, icemen have been used in ads over the past century to sell everything from shoes and

When you give

today's SCHENLEY

... you <u>know</u> you're giving

the best-tasting

whiskey in ages!

BROWNIE

Christmas happiness
for that boy means
finding a

BROWNIE CAMERA

waiting for his first snapshot.

Come in and we will show you all the Brownie
family. They work like the Kodaks.

THE HARPER DRUG CO.

Are you ready for the
slush, snow and ice?

Here is something for you that is a match for any weather . . . really
appreciated at this time of the year.

Snowmen have long been featured as commercial characters to sell everything from
whiskey to cameras.

other items of clothing to cameras, anti-freeze, whiskey, soup, and tires. The song "Frosty the Snowman" has been on carolers lips since 1950 when it was written by Jack Collins and Steve Nelson, and recorded by the singing cowboy, Gene Autry. Even the song "Winter Wonderland"—another very popular holiday tune—includes a lyric reference to a young romantic couple building a snowman to pretend that he's the local minister who can marry them. Snowmen may be what children build, an expression of humanity and life, but snowmen are also familiar images at Christmas time in our culture. (The animated TV special *Frosty the Snowman* produced by Rankin/Bass actually post-dates Archie. *Frosty* first aired on TV in 1969 while Archie was created for the mall in 1968.) Snowmen are typically friendly, non-political, non-religious wintry creatures that tickle the imaginations of children. Snowmen also provide adults with a whimsical link to their own memories of childhood. It made sense in 1968 to create an all-new Christmas attraction with a character such as a snowman.

Unlike downtown's Christmas windows and the local shopping plazas' holiday events, Akron shoppers were treated to an indoor Christmas attraction protected from the cold wind, freezing rain, and icy snow. To overlook this important feature of Archie's charms is to be unaware of Northeast Ohio's unpredictable and often severe weather conditions each and every November and December.

While Chapel Hill was open for the holidays in 1966, many of the individual stores were continuing to open into and after the start of the Christmas shopping season. 1967 was the first year the mall organized a special event to kick off the start of the Christmas shopping season. That year, the mall created quite a fanfare welcoming Santa Claus into the center of mall riding atop a live elephant! It was certainly one of the most original and breathtaking arrivals of Santa known in Akron. According to the ad, the elephant was named Babe and she was the same elephant that actress Elizabeth Taylor appeared with in the popular 1954 Hollywood movie *Elephant Walk*. 1968 saw the repeat of welcoming Santa Claus at Chapel Hill Mall as he rode atop the elephant

Archie the Snowman at Chapel Hill Mall in Cuyahoga Falls, 1973. Photo: Ron Kuner, courtesy of the *Akron Beacon Journal*. Used by permission.

Babe followed by a baby elephant named Tiny Tom. What a sight that must have been! 1968 was also the first year Archie the Talking Snowman stood guard in the center of the mall.

For the next twenty years, the debut of Archie the Snowman coincided with Santa's arrival at the mall riding atop the elephant. Starting in the late 1980s, the elephant ride ceased and Santa was welcomed into the mall and to his throne by means of an elaborately staged parade with high school marching bands, clowns, balloons, and costumed characters. Before Archie was unveiled—almost always the week before Thanksgiving—large curtains were hung inside the mall to cordon off the area where Archie and his surrounding winterscape display were being installed. Archie's arrival at the mall was typically a secret—a bit of Christmas magic!

Although we know him as Archie the Snowman, he wasn't officially called that during his first years. In advertisements during the late 1960s, the mall only promoted him as the "Talking Snowman" located in the Snow Village. Eventually the ads would refer to our snow friend by the name of Archie. However, a 2000 *Akron Beacon Journal* article written by Mark J. Price credits the mall's first promotions director, Elizabeth "Libby" Buehl with the idea of Archie. The same article also asserts that the snowman was initially referred to by the colorful moniker, Archie Arctic.

Whatever name was used, Archie was under the creative direction of Chapel Hill Mall's owner and developer, Richard Buchholzer as the legend persists. Noted as a very hands-on kind of guy by those who worked under him, Buchholzer controlled the snowman's continued existence at the mall while he was in charge. Whether the original idea for the creation of the talking snowman was Buehl's or Buchholzer's, Archie has been everyone's favorite reason to visit the mall at Christmas time for decades.

If you're old enough to have stared in amazement at the frozen giant those first few years of his at Chapel Hill Mall, you would have seen a twenty-foot-tall, smiling, snowman. He's your typical three snowball-stacked snowman with buttons down his middle section. He wore a plaid scarf, a top hat, and one of his outstretched arms

ARCHIE THE TALKING SNOWMAN IS BACK, HE'LL TALK TO THE KIDDIES EVERY DAY AND HAS A SPECIAL TREAT FOR THEM IN THE EAST COURT IN OUR CHRISTMAS VILLAGE

November 24, 1973 newspaper ad for Archie the Talking Snowman.

clasped a straw broom. To some young visitors, his most prominent facial feature was two glowing, lighted eyes that flashed when he spoke. And in those first few years, Archie was surrounded by an elaborate display that beckoned the eyes to take it all in. The Snow Village, later referred to as Archie Land, was an arctic vision of pine trees, over-sized candy canes, and twinkling lights strung between holiday boughs, with animatronic animals such as deer and forest creatures, Eskimos, igloos, penguins, bears, smaller snowmen, and even elves. In the early years, Archie and his fantasy Snow Village were contained behind white castle walls with block towers and arches reminiscent of a castle in storybook fairy tale. It was a magical place—and no one in the mall walking by could resist looking over to catch a bit of the holiday splendor.

Archie's appearance changed many times over the thirty-six years of his life at Chapel Hill Mall. Part of this is due to how he was constructed but also because he was dismantled and placed in storage after each holiday season. When the mall's maintenance workers and display personal re-installed Archie each November, the reassembly and touch up of the display materials would often require additions and changes. If you can imagine all that white fluffy material used to cover Archie and Archie Land getting dusty and soiled each year and then sitting in storage for ten months, you get the idea how routine it became to add more and more white fill material to the giant snowman and his surrounding display area. According to the previously mentioned *Akron Beacon Journal* article by Mark J. Price, Archie was originally built by mall employees of "...plywood and chicken wire that was covered in cotton batten, and spun fiberglass." Ra'ul Umaña who was employed for years at the mall and used his carpentry skills on the display asserted that the first Archie was made from lath, or wooden hoops covered by cloth, that were used to construct the ball-shapes of his body. After ten years or more, the hoops were collapsing under the weight of the creature and the additional layers of cloth added year after year to look like snow got lumpier and thicker. By the late 1970s, Umaña was asked to build a more durable, second Archie.

Though the first head was kept intact, the second body was built in sections from plywood and screws to make it easy to install each holiday season. It was so sturdy, Ra'ul insisted, "you could park a Cadillac on it. I used three quarter inch plywood." This new Archie body supported incredible amounts of weight because the sections were geometric spheres that consisted of interlocking triangles of wood. The storage needs led Ra'ul to build the base of Archie with rollers to accommodate moving the wooden display back to a storage room, out of sight, until the following holiday season.

Over the thirty-six years at Chapel Hill, Archie's face and body also changed appearance. Having to pack on more "snow" or white cottony batten to cover dirty spots and fill out the snowman each year certainly explains a lot. However, some who have seen photos of Archie across the years have noticed other minor changes. Some years Archie's nose changed shape; his right arm folded in toward his chest. Other years Archie's scarf not only changed color and fabric but it was tied or folded over differently. His hat changed in appearance, and some other years the buttons on his chest number three or two and change in shape from round to square.

Other alterations occurred in the Archie Land display because each new year the display had to be recreated. Inevitably, the staff members would focus on making an attractive display—not necessarily the same identical arrangement from the previous year. These changes also helped keep visits with Archie fresh year after year. As new display items were purchased by the mall, they replaced the worn out figures and added to the overall picturesque fantasy scene. As new display pieces were added, the mall's promotional department often renamed Archie's surrounding display. For example, in 1969, the area was called "The Magic Snow Village," and in 1972, the Archie Land display was advertised by the name "Candy Land Forest." Whatever the name of the sprawling display area surrounding Archie the Snowman, the area was a fantasy exhibition of arctic enchantment and wonder.

The heavy white castle that encircled Archie Land only lasted the first decade or so. According to Ra'ul,

> "You couldn't wheel it around. It was great—it was magnificent—it had an archway that looked like Disneyland but it was very difficult to move. It was all covered in plaster and people had knocked that around an awful lot. The plaster was falling off of it and we kept patching it. For a lot of years there, the maintenance department set up Archie and they did the best they could at the time—not many of them were trained artists but they did what they could."

Another important early change concerned the bridge where children walked in order to speak with Archie. Ra'ul replaced the two-by-fours and chain platform with a safer, more structurally sound bridge with ramps, built from three sections. Putting these sections on wheels also made storage and reinstallation year after year far more plausible for the mall's staff. Ra'ul added, "… you wheel them into place and put the pins down and the boards under them so they don't roll away. And you were good to go." With Archie receiving more than twenty thousand child visitors each holiday season, safety was of course an important factor.

Archie's most bewitching quality was undoubtedly his ability to speak and engage everyone with conversation. In those first years, children stepped up to a wooden platform with a chain to address him. The friendly, gentle snowman greeted the excited little ones and asked them easy-to-answer questions such as "Are you ready for Christmas?" and "Who are you shopping for at the mall today?" Inquiries such as "What do you want for Christmas?" were usually avoided by Archie—that question was left to Santa Claus. However, sometimes Archie would ask it in order to help hesitant, shy children to express themselves. One important thing Archie offered that Santa didn't was a piece of candy. Visiting Archie meant each child got to choose a piece of sweetness to ensure that the experience lasted a little longer than their brief interaction with Archie. The candy options over the years included candy canes, gummy chews, and others.

SPOILER ALERT: Archie the Talking Snowman didn't really speak on his own. Inside Archie Land, there was a small booth, hidden in plain sight, disguised as a Christmas cottage within the display. Inside the house, an adult could sit and not only see but hear those visiting Archie. There was a small window in the house for a person to see out of and a volume control to adjust the sensitivity of a microphone used to pick up the children's voices. In fact, the person working as the voice of Archie could often hear people walking past the display—not just those on the platform. So, on slow days or when no one was in line, Archie was known to sometimes address adults coming and going in the mall, as well as store employees passing by. Whoever worked as the voice of Archie also had a button to light up Archie's eyes as he spoke. This combination of special effects, a voice, flashing eyes, and an interactive dialogue is the charm of Archie the Snowman, creating memories in the lives of Akron children for decades. More about those glowing eyes later.

If you think the most cherished of memories of Archie belong only to his young visitors, you would be completely wrong. Some of those most passionate about Archie are the adults who helped breathe life into the talking snowman over the years. During Archie's

November 28, 1974 newspaper ad for Archie the Talking Snowman.

three decades of life at Chapel Hill Mall, those who worked as the voice of Archie were hired as seasonal employees. The community members hired for this type of temporary employment were often teenagers and college kids, the retired and the elderly, men and women looking to earn extra holiday spending money, and to be fair—quite a few people looking for holiday work that was a little different, or a little more meaningful. As one former worker shared with me, "Some of us arranged our lives so that we could work that job at Christmas time—you know, I think that speaks volumes about [us]."

My research revealed that a complete list of the seasonal and temporary employees who voiced Archie is nearly impossible to compile. A number of those who were employed as the voice of Archie have since passed on. Chapel Hill Mall never anticipated the cultural impact Archie would make on Akron. The mall's ownership has changed several times over the decades, which is a challenge to record keeping. When I inquired the current mall staff about records of staff concerning Archie, I was told they didn't exist. The list of the relevant seasonal employees who provided Archie's voice going all the way back to the 1960s probably ranges from several dozen names to potentially a couple hundred names. Many of those who did fulfill this role remain some of Archie's strongest supporters and continue to feel passionate about the emotional bond they shared with children.

Of the many who have given voice to Archie, several are notable. The first voice of Archie was identified by Mark J. Price in the aforementioned *Akron Beacon Journal* article. College student Robert Koller was in need of a job during his Christmas break in 1968 and was persuaded by his father who knew the mall's first promotions director. After helping the mall's employees build Archie, Robert's role as Archie was about finding his voice. "I'd start a dialogue with somebody that was passing by," says Koller. "Or I'd be absolutely silent. Ultimately, children would wander on up and start poking around, and I'd start talking to them and catch them off guard." Robert would ask questions such as "Where are you from? How are you doing? Where are your Mom and Dad?

Are they shopping?" but he admits he also tried to entertain the kiddies by being silly and having a sense of humor. Price's article goes on to reveal that Koller went on to join the CIA—and was even part of the team that provided intelligence information to President Gerald Ford during his time at the White House. After that, Koller went on to become an aerospace investigator.

MaryLou Fogle gave voice to Archie after she retired from many years of work at a private primary school. Working at story hour in the library and as a substitute teacher, MaryLou enjoyed listening to children. With her own children in college at the time, Fogle proudly worked as the voice of Archie starting in the late '70s, returning year after year for eight years. She said "I didn't ask children what they wanted for Christmas because that was Santa's job." But MaryLou remembers asking children what their name was, and where they lived. After asking children about their siblings, she would often encourage them to be nice to their brothers and sisters, to help their parents around the house, and to be kind to everyone. She revealed to me that children would often ask Archie where he lived and what he lived in, and she would answer, "I live at the North Pole not far from Santa's Workshop in an ice castle with my mother and father." Because of the animals in the Archie Land display, children would often ask if Archie played with polar bears, seals, and penguins. And Fogle would reply that he did play with the bears and the seals but that penguins live at the South Pole! Sometimes Archie would be asked if he had any brothers and sisters, and she replied she had a cousin named Frosty. She said "…their eyes would light up and they would say they knew Frosty and saw him on TV." Fogle's experience working in an elementary school and making full use of the window in the cottage where she sat, she says she could often judge the ages of the children, and what grade they were in at school or preschool. "If I knew the kids I would say their name and what a surprise that was." She said, "I could tell by the school uniforms what school they went to and they loved the fact that I knew that." When a minister she knew entered the mall, Fogle facetiously spoke as Archie and greeted him—by name—causing him to look around for answers to the mystery before finally recognizing the booming voice behind the giant snowman! What a sense of humor.

Fogle adds that the mall management even asked her to come in early on several occasions to speak as Archie to special groups such as day care organizations, nursing home crowds, and groups of the handicapped. She shared with me how happy she was to do that. She loved listening to children so much that she even worked at Chapel Hill Mall as their Easter bunny, Chappie—a role several other Archie workers ended up fulfilling as well. Her only reason for leaving the rewarding voice work, she explains, was to take care of her own aging parents at the time.

An *Akron Beacon Journal* article from 2007 written by Kim Hone-McMahon, makes the claim that MaryLou Fogle was the first female voice of Archie. When she was initially applying for the job, the male staff member at the mall conducting the interview reminded her that Archie's voice until that point had been exclusively male. She replied, "Archie is magic. Besides, children who speak to snowmen don't care about voices." Fogle's popularity as Archie proves youngsters didn't limit their imaginations to male-only voices. However, we all know Archie's voice does matter. MaryLou's was an important one.

The man mostly closely identified with Archie the Snowman is Ra'ul Umaña, and Umaña spoke for Archie off and on for about twelve years. Umaña not only provided Archie's voice but he had a hand in hiring and training several others that worked with Archie. His dedication to Archie meant Ra'ul found additional work with the display department at the mall, bringing his carpentry skills to Archie and Archie Land while he worked at the mall. As a young man, following his military service to our country, Umaña began filling in at Chapel Hill for a friend, working as temporary help as the voice of Archie in the mid-1970s. After several years of this, Umaña was offered more responsibility to utilize his many skills, eventually hiring others to work as Archie's voice, as well as hiring the pixies—or elf assistants—who guided the children through the attraction. In addition to those roles, he helped restore and set up Archie and Archie Land each holiday season. Umaña's

November 26, 1981 newspaper ad for Archie the Talking Snowman, Santa's arrival by elephant, as well as his Rocket Ship home, and "CHAPO" the gift-selecting computer.

machinist training also served him in carpentry, and he used his know-how to build a new Archie for the mall in the late 1970s or early '80s, when the first Archie structure was collapsing.

Knowing he wasn't the first Archie, Ra'ul admitted "...there were a couple of really good Archies before me." Explaining the particular charm of Archie, he replied,

> "I never used a falsetto voice. I used my natural voice and I didn't try to convince them that I was anybody other than exactly who I am. I talked to kids straight forward. They're real human beings. They're a lot smarter than people give them credit for. They get it. They know when they're being talked down to. And a lot of them came back."

Another skill possessed by Umaña that he brought to the voice of Archie was the ability to offer holiday greetings in several languages besides English. He told me that at times, he used little bits of Spanish, French, Japanese, Korean, and even Hindi when he addressed children at the mall as the snowman.

> "Archie's ears were much more sensitive than people thought. They were as sensitive as I wanted them to be. I had a volume control. So if I'm bored, I often listen to people talking on the bridge or halfway down the aisle. It's easy enough to tell when somebody's not speaking English. So if you listen long enough, sometimes you can pick out what language it is. If it's close enough to Spanish then you can get away with a couple of Spanish words."

Umaña remarked that his boss Mr. Buchholzer at the mall had instructed him that when he spoke as Archie not to push any particular religion because of the mall's diversity. Saying "Happy Holidays" and even addressing children in their native tongue was a way to include everyone in the spirit of the season.

A particularly delightful surprise came when Archie addressed Japanese children in their native language. Umaña had spent two years of his military service in Okinawa and picked up pieces of the language. He also admitted that he delighted in seeing the warm looks on children's faces when he could greet them in their native tongue. This encouraged Ra'ul to approach recent immigrants in Akron, asking them to teach him a few words he could use at Christmas time when he worked as Archie. That is how he picked up a bit of Hindi.

Starting in the mid-1970s, Chapel Hill hosted a popular International Festival, an event that welcomed people of all nationalities to celebrate the diversity of our residents. The festival would be an annual event at Chapel Hill Mall during the holidays for years to come. It also encouraged children of all nationalities and faiths to visit Archie in the mall's center. The opportunity to engage children from diverse backgrounds was one that Ra'ul clearly cherished in his time as Archie.

Jammin' Paul Hively, the guitarist in the house band at the Main Street Saloon, is also known as Santa Claus around Akron. His snow white beard and belly make him a natural for the Christmas time role he's played in many locations, including Chapel Hill Mall.

He got his start as the mall's Santa only after working as the voice of Archie. Hively shared with me that he spoke for Archie for one year in the 1990s before being offered the role of the mall's Santa. As Archie, he asked the children "are you ready for Christmas?" knowing that only Santa asks what children would like to find under the tree. Hively said it was fun playing an imaginary creature like Archie—the kids were always excited and they would be filled with energy as they waited in line to step up to the microphone. Playing Santa Claus at Chapel Hill Mall, he soon learned, had its challenges. Sometimes when Santa asked the youngsters what they wanted for Christmas, they were hesitant to reply since they already told Archie what they wanted, and it was frustrating! Paul also found that kids often wanted candy from Santa Claus but he had to explain that only Archie gave out candy!

Another notable person who provided Archie with a voice was Greg Berg, who spent one season in the late 1970s speaking for Archie. After graduating from North High School's radio and TV workshop, and landing another job in local talk radio, Greg looked forward to gaining more experience by creating a voice for Archie. After these valuable experiences, Greg moved to Hollywood to pursue more professional voice work and has been making a career at it ever since! Greg Berg not only found work as Fozzie Bear and Scooter on the animated TV series *Muppet Babies,* made by Jim Henson Productions but he has since worked on the movie *Toy Story* and *The Simpsons* as well. Today, he continues to work in the voice industry in animated features and in video games.

In 1979, a staff writer working for the *Akron Beacon Journal* even took his turn sitting in the booth, providing the voice of Archie. Reporter Mark Faris climbed inside the little booth to take the microphone and described his experiences in a newspaper article that ran in December 1979. Though he claimed he was nervous, and was most frightened of saying the wrong thing at the wrong time, he eventually found the experience enjoyable. Faris claimed his sense of humor helped ease the tension and he was delighted to see how children were so awestruck by Archie. Although Faris may have been intimidated by the responsibility, most of those

I've talked with who spoke for Archie describe it as an uplifting and joyful experience.

Years later, popular *Beacon Journal* columnist and author David Giffels also took his turn for an afternoon speaking for Archie. "The rules were simple: Don't make promises that can't be kept. Help them believe in something. Offer a piece of candy," stated David about his voice adventure.

Not everyone who worked as Archie was as successful as previous Archies. Alex Dorko shared his comically short-lived experience as Archie in 1999, when he was still in high school. Alex had grown up frequently visiting Archie and was surprised at how easy it was for him to get the job as the voice of Archie. "I had gone from a total nobody to Legendary Mall Voice Talent in less than an hour." Dorko continued,

> **As a teenager in the late '90s, my idols were of course Adam Sandler and Jim Carrey. Therefore, my unique Archie voice was a mix of the two, complete with hilarious well-timed outbursts of gibberish and catch phrases that I figured the giant acrylic snowman should adopt. I was the most annoying Archie the Snowman ever.**

His story continues with a description of his downfall. Alex said that late one evening in December, after almost all the kids were gone and few shoppers were left in the building, he grew bored and began to push the envelope by calling out to anyone passing by to step up to the microphone to talk to Archie. Eventually an employee from one of the neighboring businesses walked over and spoke into the mic. She told him the noise he was creating had become annoying to the other employees in the mall and kindly asked if he would stop. Instead, Alex tried to be funny and took the joke further. Dorko as Archie said, "Where do you work again? Oh, Alvin's Jewelers? I didn't know you hated Christmas over there. Attention mall shoppers, it has come to my attention that Alvin's Jewelers hates Archie, and therefore hates Christmas." Let's just say that was Alex's last day at work as the voice of Archie! The next summer Dorko joined the army. "Probably what I needed," he quipped.

The list of people who were passionate about their work with the mall's snowman also includes the pixies, or helper elves, hired by the mall as seasonal workers to greet and assist the children standing in line. It was also their role to distribute pieces of candy to children after they met Archie. Heather Quinn worked as a pixie for about five seasons in the late 1990s at Chapel Hill Mall. Quinn had been lucky enough to visit Archie when she was a little girl, so she knew it would be a good job for her as a teenager. "I have lots of good memories with Archie" Heather repeated again and again to me referring back to her time on the job. She fondly remembered greeting approaching youngsters and escorting them to the microphone. After their conversations with Archie, she helped them select a piece of candy, usually tootsie rolls, or gummy drops. Heather also remembered the Archie Land display quite well, describing mechanical elves, penguins, a pond with ice skaters, and deer whose heads lowered as if eating from the ground. The glittery, cottony material that was used to create the look of snow around Archie floated off the display and Quinn remembered frequently picking up the fluffy stuff and returning it behind the display barriers. Like MaryLou Fogle, Heather loved her job so much she too worked at spring time as the mall's Easter Bunny.

Terrie Moeller also worked as a pixie and reminisced about her experiences from the two years in the early 1990s when she worked at Chapel Hill Mall. Moeller got her job because she was a part of Chapel Hill Mall Teen Trendsetter Board. Membership included opportunities for local teenagers to model in monthly fashion shows, to perform as live mannequins in store windows, and other public relations/advertising for events at the mall. Terrie recalled her pixie costume was a green jumper, essentially a felt potato sack with neck and arm holes. She also wore a red turtleneck, red tights, and red slipper socks. "It was like walking around in old comfy pajamas" Terrie said. Heather Quinn noted that the elf costumes were in tatters by the time she was hired, so she made her own. Quinn remembered making a red and green felt jumper under which she wore a turtleneck and leggings or tights too. On her feet, she made slippers with jingle bells and also wore a jingle bell necklace.

Moeller remembered filling in for the voice of Archie when the man inside the booth would take his breaks or leave for the day. She remembered awkwardly replying "Um, I have a cold!?" to youngsters puzzlements about why Archie sounded like a girl. But mostly, kids were in such awe of Archie and his impressive size. She reported that children were excited during their time with Archie, excited being a word most everyone has used to describe Archie's young visitors. Heather Quinn shared that she remembered teenagers would also stop by the display. While visiting the mall, giggly teenage girls and sometimes even teenage boys dared each other to go up the bridge to talk to Archie. The teens tried to act cool and laughed but it was clearly still an enjoyable moment for those caught between childhood and the adult world.

With the hundreds of thousands of visitors to Archie over his decades-long lifetime at the mall, there are still treasured memories of outstanding moments over the years. Heather Quinn fondly remembered hearing Umaña speaking for Archie addressing Latino children in Spanish, and how happy the surprised children were to hear their own language. Quinn also shared that she remembers quite a few developmentally disabled children visiting the smiling snowman and how these visits formed some of her warmest memories. The special needs children would often light up when they spoke with Archie. Heather remembered one little girl who was a little shy at first when she came across the platform, but by the time she left, the little one was very happy and hugged her. It was an especially sweet and meaningful moment for Quinn.

A visitor named Kristen shared a touching story from her own childhood with me for this project. She remembered standing in line to see Archie in the early 1990s.

> "...I made my way to the microphone alone while my mom and brother waited for me on the other side of the bridge. My mom said that when Archie began speaking that it was obviously a young teenage boy who was working that day. Archie asked me if I had been a good girl and he asked

what I wanted for Christmas. My mom said I stepped right up to the microphone and said 'All I want for Christmas is for my brother to be able to walk.' My brother has cerebral palsy and cannot walk or talk, so sitting at the end of the bridge was my older brother in his wheelchair. My mom said a gasp went up all around us from everyone waiting in line as the young boy voicing Archie stumbled over his words and said 'Well, I don't know if that will be possible and I can't make any promises, but I will talk to Santa for you. Is there anything else you would like?' And I said 'No, that's all I want.' My mom said Archie let out a little sob as he said goodbye to me and I walked down the ramp and hopped up onto my brother's lap. Needless to say, I'm sure I ruined that poor boy's holiday season. Out of the mouths of babes!"

I joked a little with her about this story and Kristen acknowledged that she probably traumatically pulled everyone's heart strings on that day, many years ago.

Ra'ul Umaña remembered a sad day when he was speaking as Archie.

"…a kid came and Archie asked him what he'd like for the holidays and the kid tells me he wants his mommy back. I didn't know if he meant back from the store or where—I asked one more question and I shouldn't have but he said they buried her. Archie replied, 'I can't help you with that, son.'"

But clearly, the vast majority of memories of Archie are pleasant ones. Umaña shared another with me. "

A man came back to the booth, knocks on the door, and says he'd like to do something—'I want to propose to my girlfriend as Archie!' She came up to the platform and said 'Hi Archie!' and he said 'Will you marry me, honey?' It worked out—she said yes."

Is it possible they asked Archie to perform the ceremony?

While Archie's immense size and magical ability to speak impressed most children, others were frightened by him. In fact,

I myself was one of the children who was taken to visit Archie in the early 1970s, and year after year I was too scared to step up to the platform and address the frozen giant. Since I started researching and writing this project, several people have confided in me that they too were horrified by Archie's flashing, glowing red eyes and disembodied voice, making it impossible to enjoy the mall's Christmas attraction. My instant reassurance that I too was frightened by Archie usually brings relief to these folks who often feel as if no one could possibly understand their childhood nightmare. But I get it.

Others confessed to me about being terrorized by Archie "the Snow Monster," as one anonymous woman called him. "His eyes tripped me out. His eyes look like those cats' eyes when they get caught in the camera's flash or by glaucoma" she added. Even former *Beacon Journal* columnist David Giffels referred to Archie as "Archie the Vaguely Frightening Giant Snowman" in a 2002 article. Author and former *Cleveland Scene Magazine* writer, D.X. Ferris, shared,

> **"Let's face it: cute as Archie is, there's something ominous—in a cool way—about a 20-foot-tall snowman with red eyes and a booming voice. Santa Claus is not the most cuddly figure in the world, especially when you're a toddler. Now imagine being four and looking up at a crimson-glaring snowman the size of a building. Archie would intimidate Krampus himself."**

Bob Ignizio, founder and writer of *Cleveland Movie Blog,* explained to me that he fondly remembered visiting Archie the Snowman, "I guess the best way to think about it was as an insurance policy. If Santa somehow forgot what you asked for, surely Archie would remember." Continuing, Ignizio explains,

> **"What makes Archie so special? He's a giant talking snowman with glowing red eyes! That's all you really need…if there are some kids who are scared to sit on Santa's lap, Archie is even more potentially terrifying. So if you were cool with Archie, on some level it meant you weren't a little baby."**

November 20, 1997 newspaper ad for Archie the Talking Snowman.

When I brought up Archie's frightening eyes to Ra'ul Umaña during one of our interviews, we both enjoyed a laugh and he shared with me, "It's not my fault. I wanted blue eyes! I swear to god, I wanted blue eyes! I even went to the point of taking a chance on losing my job over it." Explaining further, Umaña recounted a story about trying to convince his boss Richard Buchholzer to change Archie's eye color because the red eyes were frightening children. "Mr. Buchholzer had already made it clear that he was never going to let me change that color and I argued with him consistently for five years. Finally I took it into my own hands." Buchholzer rented a scissors-jack every year to install Archie and decorate the inside of the mall. After everything was finished, Umaña said he used the lift one last time to swap the red light bulbs in Archie's eyes for blue ones and then put away the scissors-jack, hoping that Buchholzer either wouldn't notice or not want to bother to make a fuss about it. But Mr. Buchholzer insisted that Ra'ul get the machine back out and re-insert the red bulbs for the blue ones. In the end, the mall's owner/manager had his own vision of Archie, and he always got his way.

Maybe Mr. Buchholzer knew what Charles Dickens knew—that Christmas time is filled with all sorts of experiences, even ones that thrill and frighten us. Charles Dickens wrote the world's favorite holiday story, A Christmas Carol, as a story about Ebenezer Scrooge who is visited by four ghosts. Is the feeling of being frightened all that dissimilar from being excited—the most frequently used word to describe the children during their visits to Archie?

In addition to organizing an annual Santa Claus parade as part of the kick off event which unveiled Archie, the mall also promoted Archie in other ways. To encourage more visitors to the new attraction in 1969, Chapel Hill Mall placed a full sized, pull-out coloring page of Archie the Snowman in the Akron Beacon Journal. The poster was an illustration of the giant snowman depicting him holding a broom with one hand and tipping his hat with the other. Archie has his typical giant smile, a striped scarf around his neck, and warm, bulbous eyes. The poster appeared as a part of that year's Chapel Hill Mall shopping guide for the stores inside the shopping complex. In 1978, Archie's eleventh year at the mall, the Akron Children's Theatre Group Inc. presented several special staged performances of Archie and the Last Christmas Gift Production at the mall during selected days. In 1979 another stage play was presented to honor our favorite wintry friend. The Children's Theatre Production staged an all new story, Archie and the Lost Christmas Card for audiences throughout December that year.

Archie didn't just amuse children, he remained the topic of conversation for teens as well. When Archie was twelve years old and the first generation of his fans were about high school age, the talking snowman was covered by a story in Akron's East High

School newspaper, *The Caravan*. In that December 19, 1980 story, teen journalist Georgia Maistros documented a typical conversation between the interactive snowman and a five year-old named Jennifer. Maistros also described the secrets behind Archie's voice, proving that no one truly outgrows a curiosity about the magic of the holiday season.

The Christmas season of 2003 at Chapel Hill included Archie the Talking Snowman for the thirty-sixth year in a row. Promotions for Archie were at an all time low with barely a mention throughout the entire months of November and December in the local newspaper. Archie's popularity had seen better days—and so had Chapel Hill mall. Consumer habits were in flux in 2003. Shoppers were more likely to seek discounts and comparison shop for holiday gifts online. Not only were people shopping with their home computers but savvy shoppers were going to the brick-and-mortar stores and using mobile phones to see what lower prices were available elsewhere. Not only was this a new way of shopping in 2003—compared to ten years earlier—but it was unimaginable to those living in 1968 when the Christmas attraction, Archie the Snowman was conceived as a means to bring people into the mall. People found fewer and fewer reasons to leave their homes to go Christmas shopping. The impact was felt in Akron's plazas and malls, and it also made Christmas attractions irrelevant. Although no one realized it at the time, the Christmas season of 2003 would be the final year of Archie at Chapel Hill Mall.

November 29, 1928 newspaper ad for the M. O'Neil Co. This ad ran during the first holiday season in their magnificent new building on South Main Street.

THE STORY OF ARCHIE THE TALKING SNOWMAN

RETAILING RIVALS

Akron's rich history of Christmas attractions evolved and developed in an environment of intense competition between retailers—first, among store owners downtown, later by retailers in plazas and indoor shopping malls. In fact, a discussion of the history of the major local retailers in Akron will be helpful to understand the complexities and the competition that existed between these rivals during the annual Christmas shopping seasons.

The department store known as O'Neil's began humbly as the joint venture of Michael O'Neil and I. J. Dyas, who opened their dry goods store at 114 East Market Street in 1887. In those days, Howard Street was the dominant business thoroughfare. Polish immigrant Abraham Polsky was already open for business with his shop, Myers & Polsky, at 165 South Howard Street, having opened in 1885. Business was good for both merchants and O'Neil & Dyas moved to South Main Street in order to expand in 1889. A devastating fire destroyed the store and they rebuilt and re-opened in 1890. In 1893, Abraham Polsky, now without a partner, opened Polsky's Dry Goods and Notions in a larger building on Howard. In 1906, brothers Joseph and Charles H. Yeager bought the Dague Brothers store and took it over, ushering the start of the C.H. Yeager Co. on 56 South Main Street. By 1913, Polsky's had expanded their store into properties that covered Howard Street to Main Street. O'Neil's, Polsky's, and Yeager's were the three main rivals at the turn of the century as well as neighbors, occupying the same block for twenty years.

The development and growth of the auto industry sparked the expansion of the rubber and tire industry, which in turn fueled the city of Akron's growth. The growing rubber industry put money into the local economy and workers were shopping downtown— especially at Christmas. By the 1920s, there were significant toy departments, Christmas attractions, and Santa Clauses at not only O'Neil's, Polsky's, and Yeager's, but also Federman's, Akron Dry Goods, Central Hardware & Stove Company, Bear Furniture Company, Day Drug Company, United Dollar Store, Epp's, Dodge's, Woolworth's, and Reliable Furniture Company.

In 1928, O'Neil's moved into a new behemoth of a building further south on Main Street and their competitor Polsky's soon followed in 1930, opening their own giant store directly across the street. 1928 also saw Akron Dry Goods move to a new location that was three times larger than their original store. And in 1931, Yeager's chose not to move but rather to continue to meet their customers' demands by expanding where they were—even taking over Polsky's former building. The crash of Wall Street and the following era of The Depression affected Akron as it did everywhere else in the country. However, most of the plans for expansion by these major retailers were already underway when the crisis first hit. Although belt-tightening measures affected everyone, including the downtown stores, prices remained reasonable and the enduring retailers weathered the economic hardships.

Manufacturing was strong during the war years in Akron, and the surrounding neighborhoods and suburbs expanded in development. In order to attract customers from the growing suburbs in the 1940s, O'Neil's began building branch stores in outlying communities. By the 1950s, an explosion of shopping centers and plazas developed outside the city's retail center. By 1953, there were seven O'Neil's stores throughout Northeast Ohio, and Wooster-Hawkins Plaza in South Akron and State Road Shopping Center in Cuyahoga Falls were both open. Ten years later, these stores were joined by Barberton's Magic City Shopping Center, Arlington Plaza, Fairlawn Plaza, Coventry Plaza,

Eastgate Shopping Center, Akron Square, Midway Shopping Plaza, Lakemore Plaza, Norton Village, and more throughout the four corners of greater-Akron area.

The expansion away from the city's center also brought the development of indoor malls. In 1965, Summit Mall opened in Fairlawn as the area's first mall. This was soon followed by Chapel Hill Mall opening in 1966 on the city's northeast side. Belden Village opened in 1970 in Canton, close enough to appeal to South Akron residents. And, eventually Rolling Acres—Akron's largest mall, located on the southwest side, opened in 1975. Shopping was easy, convenient, and close-by no matter where you lived. Instead of shoppers making a deliberate journey downtown to see what the major department stores stocked on their shelves for Christmas gifts, people more easily drove, and found free, abundant parking at a strip of smaller stores or at the mall in a neighborhood closer to home.

The effects of this competition were felt immediately by downtown retailers. During the holiday season of 1958, Federman's after fifty-four years advertised their going out of business sales. In 1959, the once prosperous Yeager's went bankrupt. Although the third largest downtown department store was bought by another company, it only stayed open for two more years before finally shutting its doors. One bright spot was Quaker Square, the complex of boutique shops that opened in the renovated Quaker Oats factory downtown in 1975. Unfortunately, the presence of Quaker Square wasn't enough to bolster the failing downtown shopping district.

During the holidays of 1978, Polsky's display windows sat empty. The department store that was a downtown institution for more than ninety years closed at the end of the year. Although the store's years-long decline didn't catch anyone by surprise, the closing was an emotional one for Akron residents who had already seen far too many businesses closing in recent years. Many people blamed the employees' union or Allied Corp.—Polsky's owners— but the truth was that consumer habits had changed and shoppers didn't come downtown anymore. In January 1989, O'Neil's saw the same fate. While the branch stores were converted to May Company department stores, the downtown flagship store was shuttered after 102 years of business.

Akron suffered a devastating blow when the rubber industry's tire makers moved manufacturing to other states and out of the country. But another change in consumer habits dealt a far harsher blow to area retailers. National box stores and online shopping have made not just local department stores obsolete but they've made shopping malls struggle to stay afloat as well. The rise and fall in Akron's Christmas cultural heritage is a direct result of the competition between retailers and the changes in consumer habits over the past one hundred years.

FROSTED WINDOWPANES: DOWNTOWN WINDOW DISPLAYS

During the early days of retailing in Akron, window displays were a common sight and experience. Nationwide, retailers had been utilizing window displays since the Victorian era. One hundred years ago in Akron, residents were already familiar with window shopping and stores were maximizing their windows at holiday time for Christmas displays. The earliest holiday displays were sale items and merchandise with perhaps a bit of festive trim. Later, windows became more complex and extravagant, especially toy windows that often included moving, spinning, and leaping toys—and display figures within merchandise displays. By the post-WWII era, windows were solely devoted to entertainment purposes such as mechanical figures and enchanted fantasy scenes. It's worth noting that the experience of enjoying Christmas window displays in Akron, even ones merely filled with merchandise such as a collection of fancy dolls and elaborate toy train exhibits, is a Christmas tradition that is older than anyone currently living.

The purpose of window displays was never very subtle. Merchants were in the business of selling products. They used their windows to show off their merchandise and to lure shoppers into the stores. Although many people take it for granted that twenty-first century Christmases are commercial, it should be noted that Christmas was commercialized throughout the entire previous century as well.

SHOP EARLY!

We all feel rushed each holiday season and hear complaints of the Christmas shopping season starting too early. However, you may be surprised to learn that the start of the Christmas shopping season in Akron has begun the day after Thanksgiving for more than one hundred years! This means stores advertise their Christmas sales and special events before Thanksgiving to help shoppers prepare.

For more than one hundred years, the newspapers have encouraged people to shop early as a benefit. A 1911 ad explained the benefits of shopping early for Christmas which included choice selections, fully stocked shelves (especially in the days before modern transportation and warehouse stores), no crowds, shorter lines at counters for customer service and assistance, and more time for careful selection of gifts. Another ad, one by Yeager's in 1910, urged Akronites to shop early for their holiday gifts citing the benefits to the store sales staff and delivery men. Shopping early not only relieved the stress of the hardworking store employees but shopping early allowed them to receive their pay in a timely manner to in turn, allow them time to shop for their families. Also, retailers know that the earlier a shopper begins buying for Christmas, the more he or she is likely to spend during the season.

Where Thanksgiving day falls on the calendar is a major factor, determining when most consumers start their holiday shopping and when stores schedule ads about their holiday goods. After the Civil War, Thanksgiving was celebrated on the last Thursday in November. Unfortunately, when the holiday fell as late as November 30th, there were only twenty-four days left to shop for Christmas. In 1941, President Roosevelt signed into law that Thanksgiving would be celebrated the fourth Thursday of each November to help guarantee stores have ample time—between four and five weeks—to sell Christmas goods, and to help stabilize the economy. Since Christmas shopping accounts for a major potion of all goods purchased in the United States, an adequate holiday shopping season means a more prosperous and stable economy.

Window displays were just one means by which retailers reached out to potential shoppers to bring them into the stores. Holiday shopping was encouraged by retailers with a combination of sales and discount offers, festive decorations and trimmings throughout the store, opportunities for kiddies to meet and greet Santa Claus, walk-through Santa Land experiences, special events, celebrity appearances, and more. Competition over shoppers developed between rival merchants first in downtown Akron and later between the downtown department stores and the shopping centers, plazas, and malls as they sprung up all over town. The earliest examples of this rivalry and competition can be seen in the ever escalating elaborate designs and space used in storefront windows. Although the frontrunners in the Akron Christmas window display contest were the stores Yeager's and O'Neil's, later the rivalry to watch was between O'Neil's and Polsky's.

Whether the windows belonged to Yeager's, O'Neil's, Polsky's or another retailer, the most popular scenes depicted year after year include Santa with his elves in the toy workshop, circus and big top scenes with clowns and animals performing tricks, forest animals romping in the snow preparing for Christmas, and kitchen scenes of elves baking delicious cookies and cakes or animals making giant-sized candies. What follows are the highlights of downtown store window displays over the eight decades they were created.

Yeager's

The very first year that an Akron store promoted their Christmas windows was 1915 by The C.H. Yeager Company. That first ad encouraged Yeager's shoppers to come see Santa Claus in their front store windows at a specific date and time. While it's not exactly clear from this ad's description whether the Santa Claus was either a live person or an inanimate display item, what is clear is that store windows and their contents were important attractions to bring shoppers to the stores—so much so that Yeager's was willing to pay for advertising space to promote what was happening in their windows rather than simply list available merchandise or promote a new sale. However, Yeager's holiday windows most probably also contained a display of toys surrounding the jolly fat man.

The 1920s were a time of great expansion for retailers in downtown Akron and the competition over customers at holiday time was heating up. A 1924 Yeager's ad read, "Bring the children…and see Santa Claus in his Workshop in Yeager's window." Clearly, the store was decorating their windows not just with Santa but also a display that looks like his North Pole toy factory. The following year, Yeager's Christmas window displays incorporated a new theme: Mother Goose characters. In another leap, it is obvious from the ad description of "characters in action" that these Mother Goose decorations were indeed a moving display. And in 1926, Yeager's once again advertised Santa Claus in their holiday window displays, "When he isn't making toys in the window—he is greeting his friends in Toyland." This delightfully reminds folks that Santa is not only to be seen working in his workshop in Yeager's front windows but that children can come inside and speak to the great, jolly one inside the festively decorated toy department as well. This annual tradition of a lavish use of window space was the beginning of a most cherished Akron tradition—an excuse to press your face against the glass and stare in amazement into store windows at Christmas time.

Another highlight of Yeager's store holiday window displays occurred in 1949. Yeager's placed a Santa Claus in one of their Main Street windows that was decorated as a post office. Children were invited to write their letters to Santa, drop the envelopes in a slot in the window in front of the store, and watch the letter pass along on a conveyor belt to arrive in front of Santa inside the post office. Each letter would receive a reply from Santa, the store promised. The fun and interactive window design was created by a leading, national window design firm, Bliss Display Company. The "trick" of the display was that the letters children inserted into the window slot were deposited and held in a bin. The conveyor belt continuously circulated the same letters—not

November 24, 1949 newspaper ad for Yeager's. The illustration on the top left (just below Santa) features the holiday store window which incorporated a post office theme, complete with moving conveyor belt, and a store Santa who "answered" letters deposited by children at the store.

the individual envelopes from spectators! Bliss sold this particular holiday window design to stores all over the country.

O'Neil's

Yeager's biggest competitor at Christmas was O'Neil's store. O'Neil's first advertisement that acknowledged Christmas window displays was placed in a 1925 local newspaper and it incorporated the image of a crowd of people gathered around, gazing at a Santa Claus in the window. The race for domination in capturing the attention of Christmas shoppers with decorated Christmas windows was on. A 1926 ad by O'Neil's made the point that the holiday windows were filled with decorative display pieces, such as a Santa figure as well as toys. "Santa Claus has arrived. Our entire Main Street front is filled with the most wonderful of toys," their ad read. The toy window display is further described to include Santa Claus in his workshop, animals, clowns, and more circus-like items to enjoy.

"There's a big, fat hippopotamus that shimmies with glee— gnomes that are comical, funny and wee; busy at benches and smiling with glee—making all kinds of toys for kiddies to see. A silvery seal with a ball on his nose; a clown and a dog like you see in big shows. The clown with an elephant, that's playing a drum; a dog with a cube adds much to the fun. The sailor and cop, to please kiddies and Pop. Come early to see them—no reason why not."

The following year, in 1927, O'Neil's windows were filled with a circus-themed moving display including clowns, performing animals such as seals balancing balls, hippos, and other exotic animals. Another window is described with what we now would consider a culturally insensitive display of a jazz band "where five jolly darkies make music with glee." Unfortunately, similar racist imagery was fairly common in the 1920s. Most of the downtown retailers during this time all had toy window displays, showing off the moving, jumping, chugging, spinning, spring-loaded and steam toys that filled their toy shelves inside the store. O'Neil's continued to refer to their special Christmas displays as "toy windows" into the 1930s.

1928 was the first holiday season for the M. O'Neil Company in their new location on the corner of Main and State Street. Now with eight large showcase windows that lined Main Street, they were prepared to fill them with breath-taking, eye-catching Christmas displays to appeal to everyone. In 1928, O'Neil's windows repeated the big top theme with circus animals and other displays with all variety of animals of the forest.

The spectacular Christmas windows of 1934 at O'Neil's drew in the crowds. The display theme featured popular Walt Disney cartoon characters. In the windows that lined Main Street, children could see Mickey Mouse, Minnie Mouse, Pluto, Mickey's

THE M.O'NEIL Co

AKRON'S GREATEST STORE

O'Neil's Entire Main Street Front Is Filled With The Most Wonderful of Toys

A Thanksgiving Feast For Kiddies' Eyes

Come, little girls, and come, little boys,
To see O'Neil's windows just chuck full of toys.
In one there's a jazz band, you surely must see,
Where five jolly darkies make music with glee.
Clowns, clever and cunning, are such happy funsters,
They each try their best to please all of the youngsters;
One hides in a barrel and peeps out top or side,
While the one who is with him fair chuckles with pride.
And a clown with a drum and cymbals to play
Has a great gray goose in garments quite gay.
Two sleek black seals do tricks quite worth while
and the clown who trains them gives a pleased, prideful smile.
Then there's the fifth clown with a mammoth, bright top
That he spins round and round, with never a stop.
A queer little man whose vest won't stay down
Just knows that he'll be the talk of the town.
A shimmying "hippo" that giggles and grins
His share of laughs and praises sure wins.
So bring all the kiddies and come to O'Neil's;
There's a world of fine toys that each window reveals.

November 23, 1927 newspaper ad for M. O'Neil Co.'s window displays.

friend Horace Horsecollar, Clarabelle Cow, and more, as moving mechanical figures. In 1934, O'Neil's Disney character windows included several distinct scenes, each depicting a story. In one, Mickey, Minnie, the Big Bad Wolf, the Three Little Pigs, and others were seen dancing to a tune played by Santa Claus. Another scene depicted the wedding of Mickey and Minnie, and another window showed the Big Bad Wolf chasing after Goldilocks. Other scenes included Mickey indulging in sweets at an ice cream shop, Mickey and Minnie hard at work in Minnie's beauty shop, Mickey making candy, Mickey trying to catch a fish, Mickey and Minnie at a doll store, and Mickey working as a blacksmith. Another O'Neil's window included a deluxe train set and display. Of course, there was also one window dedicated to Santa Claus at home in his cozy cabin, with his reindeer making ready to start his Christmas Eve journey to deliver his toys.

The Disney display set was manufactured by The Old King Cole Papier Maché Company of Canton, Ohio. The papier maché characters were less three dimensional figures than they were bas-relief, with a one-piece simple movement. Adding to the overall Disney promotion, the display figures in the windows corresponded to a Disney-licensed toy department display and marionette puppet shows inside the store. No doubt, Barberton's own toy manufacturer, Seiberling Latex Products Company's many Disney-licensed rubber toys were also in the windows and available for sale at O'Neil's. The same Disney displays were used again at O'Neil's the following year, in 1935.

Later in 1937, Akron's downtown holiday windows recaptured a bit of the Disney magic. O'Neil's filled their store windows with the characters from the wildly popular animated movie of the year, announcing "The [window] scenes this year are based on Walt Disney's new picture *Snow White and the Seven Dwarfs*. See Grumpy, Sleepy, Sneezy, and the rest exactly as they'll look in Disney's picture. Come enjoy the fun." 1937's musical *Snow White and the Seven Dwarfs* was the first feature-length animated movie and the beginning of Walt Disney's legacy as a Hollywood legend. During the holidays in 1938 and 1939, O'Neil's once again

November 25, 1935 newspaper ad for O'Neil's Disney-themed windows and walk-through submarine attraction.

filled their windows with popular Disney cartoon characters—adding the Warner Bros. Looney Tunes character Porky Pig. A newspaper ad during Thanksgiving week of 1938 read, "It's an Akron tradition on Thanksgiving—Bring the children downtown to see [the windows]." The store's new tradition—just a few years old—of premiering their windows on Thanksgiving night would become a decades-old, well-established tradition for local residents.

LocaLLY MaDe TOYS

Akron's long history of tire manufacturing helped it to earn the title the Rubber Capital of the World. The rubber industry in Akron was far more than just tires—Akron was a leading manufacturer of rubber toys for many years as well. A few highlights of the locally made rubber toys and local toy manufacturers informs the curious about the content of Christmas toy displays in Akron's downtown department stores' windows.

At the turn of the twentieth century, children were playing with solid rubber figures called Brownies. Sold at the Akron Rubber Store at 223 South Howard Street downtown, Brownies were rubber characters that were sold in sets of ten or purchased individually.

Miller Rubber Products made baby dolls and rubber balls. O'Neil's, Polsky's and Yeager's all carried Miller's soft rubber My Dolly dolls. Other rubber dolls and doll parts were manufactured here and shipped to other places in the country for assembly and sold under another company's name. For example, the hot Christmas doll of 1937 was the Dy Dee Doll which was manufactured here and sent elsewhere for assembly. Also, Goodyear and General both made balloon tires for coaster wagons for a time.

Sun Rubber Company in Barberton was one of the leading toy manufacturers in the country. Sun began with making rubber accessories for baby dolls such as hot water bottles and toy bath tubs to eventually specialize in making baby dolls, rubber toy cars, and squeaky animal toys. Sun Rubber made more than five million toy automobiles in 1935 alone. After World War II, Sun Rubber made many rubber toys including animal and character squeaky toys and the first mass-produced rubber African-American doll, Amosandra, a baby doll tie-in the popular radio program *Amos 'n' Andy*.

In the 1930s, Seiberling Latex Products also started making toys

Seiberling Latex Products Disney Toys on display at The American Toy Marble Museum in the Akron History Exhibit at Lock 3. Photo: Dominic Caruso.

in Barberton. Seiberling acquired a Disney license to make Mickey Mouse toys in 1934. Soon after they also made Warner Brothers' Porky Pig toys. The Disney licensed toys made by Seiberling Latex may have been in the Walt Disney's Mickey Mouse themed Christmas windows at O'Neil's in 1934 and '35. When Seiberling Latex eventually began making *Snow White and the Seven Dwarfs* rubber toy sets, they too may have been sold at O'Neil's in the late '30s to correspond to their Christmas windows too.

Dietrich G. Rempel worked for Sun Rubber until the 1940s when he struck out on his own to start rubber toy company, specializing in hollow bodied rubber character figures. Rempel Manufacturing toys grew to be one of the largest businesses to manufacture rubber toys in the country.

Although not a rubber toy company, Saalfield Publishing was another important manufacturer. The Akron company not only published educational and entertaining children's books but also coloring books, paper dolls, puzzles and games. Formed at the

Left: Mickey Mouse toy 1950, Sun Rubber Company; **Right:** Santa 1950, Rempel Manufacturing. On display The American Toy Marble Museum in the Akron History Exhibit at Lock 3. Photo: Dominic Caruso.

turn of the twentieth century, Saalfield grew to become one of the world's largest publishers of children's books. No holiday was complete in Akron without a Saalfield book under the Christmas tree.

The war years were another time for distinctive holiday window designs at O'Neil's. Christmas 1941 brought sentimentally themed displays with scenes from an old-fashioned Christmas. "Christmas in the Gay Nineties"—a mere fifty years earlier—was a safe emotional retreat to happier times for many people that turbulent holiday just weeks after the attack on Pearl Harbor. The newspaper ad described the windows as "...reviving the spirit of an old-fashioned Merry Christmas when life revolved about the family..." capturing the safety sought in the moment. Other O'Neil's windows on Main Street that year depicted equally comforting subject matter, "The Year Round with Santa." Here, children could be amused by images of Santa tilling the ground with the assistance of his reindeer, planting tinsel and candy canes, raking up Christmas tree bulbs, and watering saplings to grow into Christmas trees. These windows demonstrated the hard work Santa does in his free time, away from his workshop, serving as a distraction from the realities of war. The safe and comforting theme was used again in 1942. Further along during World War II, O'Neil's windows in 1943 included a toy soldier parade. However, 1945's windows captured a different sentiment. One O'Neil's window depicted a scene of a father and young son reunited. This emotional scene, one can imagine, was a popular personal reminder to many of the end of the war and Akron families reunited once again.

The post-World War II era in Akron brought about a new trend in entertainment in O'Neil's Christmas windows: puppet shows. In 1946, O'Neil's windows showed off marionette performances by the Suzari puppeteers in a show entitled *Currier and Ives Ice Ballet*. In 1947, O'Neil's filled the Main and Center Street windows with the String Guild Marionettes, whose shows were performed at fifteen minute intervals, the most notable performance being *Santa's Surprise*. The following year, O'Neil's brought the String Guild Marionettes to their windows once again in a show entitled *Winter Wonderland* a story which sees "...mechanical doll houses unfolding the magic of A Night Before Christmas, the excitement of Christmas morn, clowns performing lively and amusing antics, Santa Claus and his reindeer," and more. In 1949, O'Neil's once again employed The String Guild Marionettes, produced by Wayne Reed, the same popular puppet attraction for O'Neil's windows for a third year in a row. 1949's puppet show was entitled *Puppets on Parade*. And, in 1950, the String Guild Marionettes once again returned for all-new shows with their puppets.

O'Neil's underwent a golden age of popularity in the 1950s and '60s with their Christmas window designs. Not only were budgets extravagant but nearly all the display spaces were devoted to entertainment with fantasy stories and fairytale characters instead of showcasing merchandise and goods. Across Main Street, Polsky's too was pulling out all the stops in their Christmas window displays, creating a competition for the eyes and ultimately the money of Akron shoppers.

O'Neil's downtown windows in 1953 were entitled "O'Neil's Magic Lane." The animated displays were six sequential scenes featuring a charming guide, Debbie, who led the viewers along a narrative story featuring an enchanted wonderland of toys and games, children immersed in dreams of sugar-plums, a Lionel train display, and a corner window with Santa spilling toys from his bountiful bag. In 1954, O'Neil's windows depicted another sequential narrative. Starting with the corner window on Main and State Street, the windows told the story of "The Life of Santa Claus" including Kris Kringle as a young boy.

1955 saw a wondrous animated display in O'Neil's Main Street windows as well, with the theme "Christmas in the Forest" featuring woodland creatures enjoying the spirit of the season. Next to circus displays, forest animals have been the most common and popular theme for store windows in downtown Akron. A newspaper ad by O'Neil's in 1955 pulled at adults to return to their own childhood tradition of viewing the O'Neil's Christmas window displays—an appeal to readers' emotions but also an acknowledgment that O'Neil's had been creating window attractions for thirty years—long enough for the first generation in Akron who grew up enjoying O'Neil's window displays to begin bringing their own children to see them.

O'Neil's windows at the end of the 1950s provided another highlight. The holiday windows referenced an important event happening in 1959—the territory of Alaska became a state! According to an ad in the newspaper that year,

> "Kimo invites you to see...Land of the Northern Lights. Kimo is one of the enchanting Eskimo children you'll see in our Christmas windows, this year a tribute to Alaska, our 49th state. Not only will you see these friendly, chubby, slanty-eyed little people, but also their friends in the Far North country...playful, mischievous penguins, bears, seals, sled dogs, walruses!"

This year...as every year...your Christmas begins
with the Thanksgiving window-parade past O'Neil's

O'Neil's

invites all Akron to see our wonderful animated

CHRISTMAS
WINDOWS

The dancing dolls at every trick step so please that gleeful young father-and-son team . . . as their first Christmas together in many! The performing elephants nod sympathetically at a webfeet gentleman, roll puffing from too much turkey. The tin soldiers smartly salute two passing sailors . . . and Porky Pig is definitely grandstanding for the merry little girls with their noses pressed against the window. This is the beginning of Christmas in Akron . . . and O'Neil's this Thanksgiving, considers itself much blessed to having so firm and traditional a part of it.

VISIT O'NEIL'S TOYLAND

. . . where all your good friends from "Alice in Wonderland" come to lifelike reality . . . and where Santa has a package for every good little child (all this for 24¢ and 1¢ tax). P-T Boat and Toy Auto Rides, too . . . and all the toys a child could wish for! On O'Neil's Second Floor.

November 21, 1945 newspaper ad for O'Neil's Christmas windows.

Obviously, it would also take several years before the lower forty-eight residents would become more culturally sensitive to native peoples. That same year, O'Neil's also installed a fifteen-foot St. Nick atop the store—visible to everyone on the streets downtown—to remind passersby of the spirit of the season found inside the store.

The decade of the 1960s continued the golden era of extravagant and enchanting animated window displays at O'Neil's. In 1961, O'Neil's was proud of their Christmas windows entitled "An Adventure Through Santa's Toymaker Shop." The fantasy display was "the story of two little girls who visit the Toymakers and lend their hands in painting, decorating, and repairing toys. They leave for home in a gift-laden sleigh where, fast asleep, they wait for Santa while their toy friends come to life. It's a child's dream of fantasyland come true." That same year, O'Neil's installed a new concept, Window Wonderland, in their north corner window. Customers were given the opportunity to step inside the window to shop from a specially stocked display of Christmas gifts. With access from the sidewalk, people were encouraged to step up into the little shop in the glass windows, open during regular store hours. Window Wonderland was repeated for the holiday season in 1962.

Also in 1962, a rambunctious, comic strip character came to life in O'Neil's windows. O'Neil's opened the curtains on their windows to reveal "The Wonderful World of Dennis the Menace," paying tribute to the popular daily syndicated newspaper comic strip by Hank Ketcham. Their ad read,

> **"See the neighborhood mutts get a hand-out as Dennis outwits the Dog Catcher... See the soda jerk go out of his mind at the drug store... see budding young carpenters building a precariously balanced clubhouse... see Dennis catch all the fish while Dad and Mr. Wilson fail to get a nibble... see Dennis drive everyone to distraction as he gets lost on the elevators... see Dad and Mr. Wilson making like small boys with an electric train while Dennis lurks around... See Dennis snooping through every window in the house to make sure Santa doesn't get away!"**

November 25, 1964 newspaper ad for O'Neil's Sno-People window display.

The windows included the popular characters from the comic strip including Dennis the Menace, his parents Henry and Alice Mitchell, the exasperated neighbor Mr. Wilson, Dennis' friends Margaret and Joey, and Ruff—Dennis' dog.

In 1964, O'Neil's featured adorable little snow folk in their Christmas window displays. Their ad proclaimed,

> "Little Sno-Peep and all her frosty friends have arrived on the scene at O'Neil's…direct from the Land of the Sno-People. Their merry antics will delight the young and young-at-heart tonight as they scurry and scamper thru O'Neil's Christmas windows…bringing all the joy of the season to downtown Akron."

In 1967, O'Neil's revealed their new store windows with the

Are these the Sno-People figures from the 1964 O'Neil's windows, installed at Lock 3 in 2014? Photo: Dominic Caruso.

theme, "The Littlest Angels from Around the World" featuring cute, mischievous cherubs from seven different countries. As with many of their themes, the Littlest Angels came with a whimsical back story,

> "Have you ever met a cherub? They're the littlest, roundest, most fun-loving angels in the whole entire firmament… and quite easy to recognize. In the first place, their wings are generally a little askew…or on backwards. And, due to their somewhat uncelestial behavior, cherubs are the only variety of angels that ever skin their knees. Of course, they love parties and games, raisin cookies, singing (a bit loudly, and sometimes off-key), dancing, other cherubs, and people, but…more than anything else, they love Christmas."

By the end of the decade, O'Neil's again appealed to shoppers' nostalgia at the holidays with the theme "An Old Fashioned Christmas at O'Neil's." In an ad describing their deluxe window displays, O'Neil's invited customers to imagine simpler times, saying,

> "Come one, come all on a journey into yesteryear. Over the river and through the woods, to the olden days, the golden days, we go. Back to Grandma's kitchen, warm and fragrant, to sleigh rides in the snow, to bringing home the most beautiful tree ever for your very own. Back to feather beds and fireplaces, to facts and fancies just remembered. Come back with us to long ago, when we were very young."

This appeal for a nostalgic reflection back to happier days not only fits holiday sentiments but was a popular theme used by retailers throughout the country during the darkest days of the Viet Nam War. The last time O'Neil's used this same theme was at the end of World War II, appealing to a sense of comfort during difficult times for its community and shoppers.

In 1971, O'Neil's Main Street windows were filled with lavish moving decorations exhibiting a delicious candy theme. The fantastic scene seemed straight out of *Willie Wonka and the Chocolate Factory,* depicting a candy cave, magic soda pop, candy apple trees, a peppermint grove and a gumdrop vineyard.

Despite years of success, by the 1970s the flagship store of O'Neil's was clearly feeling the absence of shoppers who were migrating to the suburban shopping opportunities. In 1972, O'Neil's filled the local newspaper with ads highlighting the unique attractions only downtown Akron offered its shoppers. The store reminded those who no longer ventured downtown as often that the store's marquee still featured the life size Nativity scene, "…an O'Neil's tradition for 17 years." The still profitable store also promoted their extravagant window displays in 1972 which again embraced nostalgic Victorian imagery:

> "Peek into a dry goods store, chuckle at a horse-drawn trolley, watch sleigh and horses being groomed for a snow-flaked trip. Join tiny shoppers in a street scene and watch youngsters crack the whip on a frozen pond. All a part of our theme of Yuletide Past…the big Victorian mansion… O'Neil's House of Christmas."

Not only were O'Neil's windows filled with the "House of Christmas" theme but their gift wrapping and packaging for the holiday season also reflected it.

During the holidays of 1978, O'Neil's biggest rival, Polsky's, was in the midst of a going-out-of-business sale and was closing by the end of the year. Throughout the 1970s, both O'Neil's and Polsky's had phased merchandise back into their holiday window displays—entertainment windows became a luxury with fewer and fewer shoppers coming downtown. Although Polsky's windows sat empty in 1978, O'Neil's was working against the same fate. With renewed vigor, O'Neil's spent $30,000 on their latest window displays composed by a national design firm. 1978's theme was gnomes, capitalizing on a popular national merchandising trend of the time. The lovable little folk filled the major display in the central fourteen-by-five-foot window at O'Neil's, as well as six other windows. The gnome trend was inspired by the best-selling picture book *The Life and Works of Gnomes* by Dutch illustrator Rien Poortvliet in collaboration with Dutch physician Wil Huygen. The gnomes windows display in Akron was just one in a national campaign that corresponded with tie-in merchandise at Christmas, and which included wrapping paper, tree ornaments, dolls, stationery, puzzles, and calendars. Although O'Neil's had hired national firms to design their Christmas windows in years before, this obvious national promotion might have amazed children but adults may have winced if they recognized how more and more national brands and identities were replacing local brands and identities. In 1979, gnomes once again appeared in an O'Neil's storefront window while other merchandise and gift ideas dominated the displays in the other windows.

Few windows were used in the early '80s for animated Christmas displays. However, in 1984 O'Neil's was re-invigorated with additional investments to not only remain open downtown but they also put money into new Christmas animatronics and display pieces for their windows. In their Main Street windows of 1984 O'Neil's unfolded a story about a new character, Happy News Boy, a scrappy 1920s-style newspaper street vendor who offered

November 26, 1978 newspaper ad for Gnome window display at O'Neil's.

uplifting headlines about the holidays. In a newspaper ad that year, O'Neil's introduced their new newsie character,

> "O'Neil's has a Christmas surprise for you. We have a new member in our family. His name is Happy™, The Happy News Boy. Happy is a magical character that brings happiness to all children in the world. He has a special gift for you. Your very own O'Neil's Happy Times News Reporter hat."

The nostalgic Depression-era Happy character was not only intended to appeal to children and play off the popularity of the Broadway show and movie *Annie*. It was probably intended to connect with the aging shoppers that still frequented the downtown storefronts as a way to have them bring their grandchildren to the store and expose the younger generation to the benefits of shopping at O'Neil's.

In 1987, O'Neil's was eager to show off the remodeling they had done and improvements made to Santa's Enchanted Forest inside the store however little was done to provide entertaining window displays. Closed circuit TV cameras were set up to transmit the sights within The Enchanted Forest on the store's third floor to TVs in the Main Street windows—so people walking by on the street could see what was happening inside the store.

Christmas in Akron in 1988 saw a repeat of the extravagance again at O'Neil's in the Santa's Enchanted Forest walk-through displays. However, business owners and city officials chipped in to make sure O'Neil's windows were full. The city of Akron pulled $11,500 from their budgets to buy a collection of animatronic displays to fill five windows, while the Akron Zoo took responsibility for decorating another window, and O'Neil's agreed to fill the seventh window. Their 1988 ad read,

> "Delight to a Victorian Christmas in all it's nostalgic splendor. Enchanting animated dolls in period costumes act out traditional turn-of-the-century holiday celebrations. You'll see St. Nicholas himself, the Snow Queen and her Prince, Bambi and his friends, and much, much more. Each lovely scene is framed in icy white branches, sparkled with lights, and the sounds of favorite Christmas carols ring through the air. The Spirit of Christmas Past is glowingly present at O'Neil's. Come. Enjoy."

This was the last Christmas O'Neil's remained open for business.

POLSKY'S

While Yeager's and O'Neil's were the first two stores to create outstanding Christmas windows to compete for Akron's shoppers in downtown, soon the rivalry between O'Neil's and Polsky's was the one that propelled greater creative output and larger budgets devoted to window displays. Polsky's was a late comer in promoting their windows as something worth coming to witness, and 1928 was the first year Polsky's advertised their own Christmas window displays. Up until then, they had largely been concerned with appealing to holiday shoppers through merchandise and toys, advertising children's winter clothing, and eventually dolls and toys. The first appearance of an ad by Polsky's to offer shoppers something to look at—a bit of Christmas wonderment with an eye-catching merchandise display—marked their entry into a hotly contested race to attract shoppers. Soon enough, Polsky's would be neck and neck with O'Neil's in their animated window displays, and their competition for shoppers resembled that of Macy's and Gimbels in New York.

Throughout the 1940s, Polsky's gained widespread attention with their annual Nativity scene, referred to as "The Star of Bethlehem" window. The Nativity window remained the same year after year while displays to entertain the kiddies were created new each season. For example in 1944, Polsky's created a series of nine displays to explain the history and origins behind our American Christmas traditions. Window gazers were promised fascinating tableaus about the popular poem "The Night Before Christmas," the origins of mistletoe, the lore behind decorating a tree, and more.

And from 1945 to 1949, Polsky's featured the Kingsland Marionettes performing in their storefront windows at intervals each day throughout the holiday season. Of course, Polsky's great rivals, O'Neil's, also featured puppet shows in their windows across Main Street during the same holiday seasons. In 1945, at Polsky's, the Kingsland Marionettes performed the archery scene from *Robin Hood,* scenes from *Alice in Wonderland* and *Humpty*

November 24, 1954 newspaper ad for Polsky's window displays.

Dumpty, six dance routines including Barnacle Bill the sailor, animals and clowns from the circus, and the *Fable of the Desert Wonder.* In 1947, The Kingsland Marionettes performed an act of a three-ring circus, complete with clowns, animals, and acrobats. In 1948, the Kingsland Marionette show was entitled *The Nativity* and told the biblical story of Mary, Joseph and the baby Jesus. Other Polsky's windows in 1948 included a display of Santa Claus seated at an organ with a choir of angels accompanying him singing Christmas carols. Apparently, those gathered around the store windows could also hear the carols and were encouraged to sing along! And, in 1949, the Kingsland Marionettes returned for a fifth year with a new circus themed production. The show included clowns, trapeze artists, elephants, lions, and bareback riders.

In their Main and Center Street windows in 1950, Polsky's featured a display of Santa and his elves watching Christmas cartoons on a giant television set! Yes, television sets were the most popular item in stores that year and for many years that followed. The newspaper of this era was filled with ads for TV sets, at various prices to suit many local families' budgets. Also in 1950, Polsky's Main and State Street windows featured an elaborate Lionel model train display, and a scene depicting Trixies—little fantasy people who help the world get ready for Christmas.

Polsky's golden era of Christmas windows exhibited an unequaled grandeur. In 1953, the store advertised many scenes in their Main Street windows including the Nativity scene with the Christ child and his mother Mary which now also incorporated speakers playing traditional Christmas carols. What a joy it must have been to stand in front of Polsky's frosted window panes gazing at the sacred story while listening to heavenly carols. This same year, Polsky's windows also featured "Angel Dolls in Paradise" with guardian angels from Heaven and dolls on display, Santa in an automobile, Santa's elves packing the sleigh, a white Christmas tree with a bounty of gifts beneath it, and circus themed scenes with clowns, giraffes, and performing dogs.

THE SINGING TOWER

Promoted as "carols from the clouds," each December in the 1930s and '40s in downtown featured music floating down from above. Traditional Christmas carols were broadcast daily from a collection of powerful loudspeakers mounted high within Akron's tallest building, the First Central Tower—what we now call the FirstMerit Building. The Singing Tower broadcast holiday music that was said to be heard over a radius of several miles from the city's center.

The music was provided by local performers located in studios within the Mayflower Hotel. The sound was then carried through wires several blocks north on Main Street to the Tower's speakers. The musical program was also simulcast on WJW radio. The performers included soloists, children and school choirs, civic choruses, glee clubs, instrumental groups, military bands, accordion groups, employee bands, and even large orchestras. For example, in 1936, Estelle Ruth, a child prodigy from Louisville Kentucky then living in Akron, played carols on the Palace Theater organ each day at noon for 15 minutes. She even solicited requests!

The Singing Tower was jointly sponsored by the Sun Radio Company and *The Akron Times-Press* from its start in 1932 and when the newspaper was purchased by its rival in 1938, the *Akron Beacon Journal* continued as the Singing Tower's co-sponsor until the late 1940s. Though each year was different, the holiday music program was generally broadcast twice a day, at noon and in the evening, for a couple hour's worth of music each day during the two weeks before Christmas.

In 1954, Polsky's filled nine Main Street windows with Christmas finery. As usual, one window featured the Nativity display with sacred music. Another window displayed a French salon for dolls and included seamstresses, wigmakers and face painters. Also, a set of windows featured Mother Goose Tales, fat cherubs, and bundles of gifts were dedicated to women's fashions celebrating the color pink. Selling ready-to-wear women's fashions had always been one of Polsky's strengths and they showed off their best at Christmas.

In 1955, Polsky's once again featured their Nativity display. They also created a sequence of displays sharing the imagery of Clement C. Moore's popular poem "The Night Before Christmas," also known as "A Visit from St. Nicholas." In other windows, Polsky's created a white fashion display filled with white lingerie, gowns, and women's wear.

Another highlight in Polsky's window displays includes 1959, the year Polsky's returned to a nostalgic theme with "A Letter to Santa" which incorporated Victorian-era settings, to help bring a sense of an old-fashioned, sentimental feeling to the holidays. The following year, Polsky's created an all-new window theme: "Santa Claus and his Toyland Circus." In a 1960 ad the windows were described as,

> **"Starring Raggedy Ann, Raggedy Andy, and Jingles the Clown. Come see their animated antics as they visit Santa's wonderful Toyland Circus…with the enormous Pink Elephant…the Raging Blue Bear, the Calico Cat and many other fascinating characters."**

And, in 1961, the Polsky's windows were filled with teddy bears enjoying the spirit of yesteryear. "Our delightful, roly-poly, fuzzy-wuzzy bears are all dressed up in "Roaring Twenties" costumes to go to the Christmas Hop," and in a 1961 ad, which continued, "See them crank their Tin Lizzie, and Charleston to Santa's jazz band. Children love their frolicsome antics, and Mom 'n Dad may find a thing or two to reminisce about! Every window is good fun… don't miss a one!" In the window on Polsky's south corner was the jolly St. Nick himself.

A twelve week Polsky's employee strike, that began in mid-September 1970 and lasted until mid-December, hampered Christmas shopping for the year. The rubber workers union asked members to honor the boycott as Polsky's store employees looked to form a union that was not recognized by store management. The conflict was deeply felt by the store as competition for loyal shoppers at Christmas time was fierce. Despite the strike, a store ad placed

Polsky's Invites You and Your Family To See Our Christmas Windows

This Year We Present For Your Holiday Pleasure . . .

"SANTA CLAUS and HIS TOYLAND CIRCUS"

Starring Raggedy Ann, Raggedy Andy, and Jingles the Clown! Come see their animated antics as they visit Santa's wonderful Toyland Circus . . . with the enormous Pink Elephant . . . the Raging Blue Bear, the Calico Dog, and the many other fascinating characters. Enjoy our Christmas Windows in the Akron Tradition . . . enter this magical Childhood Land with Ann and Andy . . . this Thanksgiving Day! Also *see* our unusual Nativity Window . . . with its exquisite Italian Imported Figures!

Christmas Windows . . . . Open Wednesday, November 23. 4 P. M.

Polsky's

POLSKY'S Salutes ATCS new METROLINER fleet of luxury coaches . . . another reason to shop in exciting downtown Akron. Rides there in regular service beginning Wednesday, November 23.

November 23, 1960 newspaper ad for Polsky's "Toyland Circus" window display.

in November 1970 confirmed that Polsky's windows were indeed decorated for the holidays, although no information about their content or theme was offered. Each following year, the window displays at Polsky's became less and less entertainment oriented and featured more merchandise, an effort to make sales a priority in order for the store to remain open.

In 1973, Polsky's windows embraced a party theme:

> "**See the new Santa surprise birthday party in our windows...Matilda Mouse decides that it would be nice if someone gave Santa a surprise party. Everyone joins in...Sarah Skunk, Chrisi Bear, Lucian Chipmunk, Lucy Goose, Sammy Porcupine, Billy Beaver, Ronald Rabbit and Charlie Chimp. Santa is indeed surprised! See this charming story unfold through the wonderful world of animation in a series of 8 delightful windows."**

Despite the obvious charm and enchantment of these windowed attractions, fewer and fewer people were shopping downtown each Christmas season.

The following year Polsky's created another sequential story in their Main Street windows. In 1974, the street level windows display told the story of the gingerbread boy. In a succession of six windows, one could see the unfolding story of Timmy the gingerbread boy who was multiplied thousands of times by the Good Fairy in order to spread Christmas joy to all the children.

The scenes of the Gingerbread boy were repeated in Polsky's windows for the next four years, through the holiday season in 1977. This was the last set of animated figures in Polsky's windows. At Christmas in 1978, Polsky's display windows sat empty while they sold off the remainder of their merchandise in preparation of closing. Although the store's years-long decline didn't catch anyone by surprise, the closing was an emotional one for Akron residents who had already seen far too many businesses close in recent years. Inside the store, departments had been reduced and even closed down over recent years. Although many people blamed the employees' union or Polsky's owners, Allied Corp., the truth was that consumer habits had changed and fewer shoppers came downtown.

AKRON HOME MEDICAL SERVICES

While O'Neil's and Polsky's were struggling to stay in business, another nearby retailer attempted to recapture some of the spirit of the season brought on by the decorated animated Christmas windows. Starting in the mid-1970s, Akron Home Medical Services, located at West Market Street and Maple Street, created heart-warming displays in their storefront windows. By 1990, after both O'Neil's and Polsky's had closed, Akron Home Medical Services was celebrating their sixteenth annual displays in seven large showcase windows with holiday scenes of spinning bears, skiers, ice skaters, and even a Nativity set. In 1992, a local photo-journalist for the *Akron Beacon Journal* captured a shot of a small child pressing his face to the glass, watching the animated display scenes. That same year, it was said that the windows were designed by an Akron Home Medical Services employee Joan Nervo and an Akron City Hospital employee Judy Csonka. A 1995 newspaper ad said, "Remember the excitement of seeing Christmas windows in downtown Akron? Relive those days now—with your family and friends at 5 Points." Clearly the decades-long custom of enjoying animated window displays had inspired others to keep the tradition alive. The last year that Akron Home Medical Services decorated their windows appears to have been 1998, ending their own twenty-plus year revival of one of our hometown's most beloved Christmas experiences.

BEYOND O'NEIL'S & POLSKY'S

Although Christmas 1988 was the last holiday season that O'Neil's store was still in business, the story of their window display pieces and the Santa's Enchanted Forest display sets doesn't end there. After the store closed in January of 1989, the remaining collection

November 23, 1989 newspaper ad for Akron Home Medical Services windows.

of O'Neil's animatronics were sold to the owner of the Carousel
Dinner Theatre, Prescott Griffith. This lot of display sets included
the The Wizard of Oz, Alice in Wonderland, Peter Pan, the fairy
tale collection of Mother Goose, 3 Men in a Tub, Three Little Pigs,
the Little Old Woman Who Lived in a Shoe, a variety of Cabbage
Patch dolls, the giant Raggedy Ann doll, a myriad of St. Nicholas
figurines depicting him from cultures around the world, and more.
O'Neil's had purchased the sets in 1984 for their Santa's Enchanted
Forest and they were valued at $50,000, however it was reported
that Griffith bought the collection for $7,500. (It is not known if
the window display pieces paid for by the city in 1988 were sold
in this lot to the Carousel Dinner Theatre or not. However, the

Wizard of Oz window display at the Polsky building in 2014. Photo: Dominic Caruso.

1988 O'Neil's window display sets did join this collection by 2005.) When Griffith's plans to build a permanent display changed, he sold the collection to the Akron Zoo in October 1989. Although O'Neil's was out of business, city and zoo workers installed the animatronic figures and display sets in O'Neil's windows for the holiday season in 1989. The Wizard of Oz set was on display at Prinz Office Equipment, at Buchtel and Main Street. For the next several Christmas seasons, the animatronic collection was exhibited at the zoo as a part of their annual holiday lights display throughout the park.

In 1997, zoo officials decided to sell the collection and the city of Akron collaborated with Downtown Akron Partnership to purchase the pieces for $14,000. For the 1997 holiday season, the collection was used to re-create an elaborate walk-though experience called Santa's Holiday Wonderland at Quaker Square. With light displays purchased from Clay's Park and dozens of decorated Christmas trees, the animatronic sets were once again brought to life and open to the public for viewing. Santa's Holiday Wonderland

Wizard of Oz window display at the Polsky building in 2014. Photo: Dominic Caruso.

Alice in Wonderland window display at the Polsky building in 2014. Photo: Dominic Caruso.

was located in the Depot Pavilion at Quaker Square—now Quaker Station at Quaker Square. A $1 donation was requested by visitors to benefit the Make-A-Wish Foundation and the attraction eventually raised more than $24,500. At Christmas in 1998, the former O'Neil's animatronics were again on exhibition at Quaker Square, however the donations this year were collected on behalf of Akron Children's Hospital.

The following holiday season, for the first time in ten years, the former O'Neil's animatronic Christmas display pieces appeared in the windows on Main Street—in the former O'Neil's department store's showcase windows. Earlier in the year, the law firm Roetzel

& Andress had occupied the upper floors of the newly renovated building but the ground floor windows remained empty—until Christmas. It was reported that more than forty thousand people visited the reinstalled window displays in 1999—a respectable number considering there was little else in downtown Akron in those days. Although many of the animatronic display sets were originally purchased for O'Neil's in-store walk-though attraction Santa's Enchanted Forest, they were now used as window displays—and continued to be referred to as O'Neil's window display collection. For the next four years, downtown once again glowed with the nostalgia of Christmases past as Akron's youngest came to press their faces against the glass and adults stopped to see a reminder of their childhoods.

In 2005, the windows in the former O'Neil's department store were no longer available due to building renovations, so seven displays of the animatronic pieces were placed throughout the Akron-Summit County Main Library. Many children visiting the library saw the moving display figures for the first time, while adults reminisced about Christmases past. By the following holiday season, the animated figures returned to downtown windows. In 2006, half of O'Neil's windows were once again filled with the much-beloved animatronic sets as well as both corner windows of the former Polsky's department store—now owned by the University of Akron—across Main Street. The use of both venues allowed the window designers to use more of the sets than usual to create the largest Christmas moving figure display since the late 1990s at Quaker Square. For the next four years, only the large corner windows of the Polsky's building were used at Christmas to exhibit the moving figures.

In 2011, Downtown Akron Partnership loaned the prized Christmas animated figures to the historic estate, Stan Hywet, located in West Akron. During the holidays of 2011, visitors to the former home of F.A. Seiberling, the co-founder of The Goodyear Tire & Rubber Company, enjoyed the sights of the popular Christmas attractions that once filled our downtown retailers. Inside the Manor House, the Wizard of Oz set was staged near the front entrance. On the mansion's second floor at the end of

Ice Princess & Prince figures on display at Lock 3 in 2014. Photo: Dominic Caruso.

the north hallway were the Ice Prince and Ice Princess. And, on the balcony overlooking the Great Room stood figures from the Alice in Wonderland set. In other rooms within the mansion were vintage toys and games accurate to the period of each room's decorations. What a grand historical Akron Christmas display that must have been. However, entry into Stan Hywet Hall and Gardens to see the displays wasn't free. Tickets were $17 each for adults, $7 for children six to seventeen years old, and only children under five years old got in free.

Once again, the Polsky's building corner windows during the Christmas season of 2012-2014 were decorated with moving figures from the old O'Neil's collection. These three years, each corner window held only one display set each—the remainder of the collection was located on exhibition at Lock 3. More on Lock 3 later.

Much labor and skill goes into designing Christmas window displays. One Akronite who knows the truth in this statement is Lawrence Nixon. Nixon went to work for Polsky's display department in 1969 and eventually was hired to work for O'Neil's as well. Driven by his passion for the department stores' Christmas decorations and attractions he enjoyed as a child in downtown Akron, he earned his living working in the field, eventually retiring from Macy's as a visual merchandising senior executive in 2008. In the early 1970s, Nixon met his wife Cynthia when they both worked for Polsky's. Together the Nixons have dedicated themselves each Christmas to recreating the impressive grandeur of Akron's Christmases past and to being the custodians of the historic pieces in the former O'Neil's collection.

In 1997, both Lawrence and Cynthia were invited to join the team of workers who designed and installed the animated Christmas display, Santa's Holiday Wonderland, set up at Quaker Square from the former O'Neil's display collection. Every year since then, the Nixons have stepped up to continue the tradition of keeping these animatronic pieces on exhibition somewhere in Akron—whether it's Quaker Square, the former O'Neil's windows, the Polsky's building windows, or elsewhere.

In addition to designing the displays, there is quite a bit of other labor and know-how required to maintain the delicate, moving figures. The Nixons have explained that each year every piece that makes up the display must be unpacked from storage. The figures' clothes must be dry cleaned and often steamed to lay correctly. Wigs and faces must be refreshed on each figure. And, repairs to fingers and feet must be attended to as well. The aged pieces in the collection must be packed away in boxes very carefully and transported in such a way to protect them. The motors for each moving piece must also be repaired, rebuilt, or rewired frequently. The animatronic figures are kept moving for long periods through the holiday season each year and the motors wear out. There are also background pieces and other display elements that accompany the moving figures, such as ground snow, Peter Pan's ship, the backgrounds behind each set, decorated Christmas trees, lights, and many more elements. All the custodial care of the vintage pieces in each set requires quite a bit of time, energy and know-how.

While trying to keep each set as authentic to the original

The sign reads:

> The Old Lady that lived in a Shoe,
> She had so many Cabbage Patch Kids
> She didn't know what to do.

Cynthia and Lawrence Nixon installing the Care Bears window display in 2010.
Photo: Shane Wynn.

designs as possible, the Nixons have tried to add different touches
to keep the displays expansive and fresh for the public. They also
worked hard to rotate the different sets for each year's window
displays so the public continues to see what is in the collection. For
example, one year the Alice in Wonderland and the Peter Pan sets
may be in Polsky's windows, but the following season, the Nixons
may use the Wizard of Oz and the Ice Princess and Prince sets.
Of course, each set includes a half dozen or more figures, clothes,
wigs, backgrounds, and other pieces. Theirs is a labor of love. In a
2006 *Beacon Journal* article about the window displays, Lawrence
Nixon said, "The only other way I would be able to do this is to be
in New York. I'm a lifetime resident, and this is the kind of thing
we want kids to have. We love Akron."

For years, the Nixons filled their team to work with the displays
with friends, volunteers and family members including their
children and grandchildren. Since the displays must be ready to
exhibit by Thanksgiving each year, the team usually begins working
in September. The long hours spent inside the cramped windows

and display spaces—sometimes without heat—takes dedication. For many years, the Nixons have spent their weeks and days in November working to design and install the Christmas windows downtown which means their own Thanksgiving dinner is sacrificed. Without the Nixons' devotion to looking after and taking care of the former O'Neil's display pieces, the glory of Akron's past Christmases would not still be with us.

We Invite You to See the Polsky Christmas Windows

In our "Star of Bethlehem" window you will catch the deep significance of Christmas, stop to rejoice again at the birth of the greatest and most honored of men.

In our "Laughing Santa Claus" window, repeated by request, you'll find the merriness that is Christmas for the children Come, stand, laugh with good old Santa.

Polsky's

November 24, 1943 newspaper ad for Polsky's "Star of Bethlehem" window display.

SACRED WINDOW DISPLAYS
OF O'NEIL'S & POLSKY'S

The two rival downtown department stores, Polsky's and O'Neil's, may have been engaged in fierce competition for shoppers' attention, however, neither store ignored the spiritual side to the yuletide season. Although most of their Christmas displays were dominated by secular displays about Santa Claus and popular fairy tale characters, both Polsky's and O'Neil's dedicated great labor and effort to include a significant amount of their limited decorative and display space to religious imagery.

During World War II, Polsky's advertised that their north corner window, at Main and Center Street (since renamed University Ave.), included a display which depicted the story of the Nativity with Mary, Joseph, the baby Jesus, and the three wise men. Also referred to as the "Star of Bethlehem" window, this reverent Nativity display reminded shoppers of the spiritual side of the holiday. The powerful and emotional Main Street sacred window display was repeated each year at Polsky's through the 1940s.

In 1948, Polsky's added another special treat. The Kingsland Marionettes once again entertained in the store's Main Street windows, this year with a performance entitled *The Nativity*. The familiar classic Christmas story was retold with puppets resembling the three wise men, Mary, Joseph and the newborn King. The puppet show started over every half hour to enthrall the youngest as well as the oldest passersby who stopped to watch.

an old Polsky custom . . .

for young and old alike, a treat as
important as the holiday season itself . . .
the opening of the always exciting . . .
always beautiful Polsky Christmas
windows, on Wednesday, Thanksgiving Eve
We invite you, as in other years, to
bring your family and enjoy the show . . .

Back Again from a Nationwide Tour

KINGSLAND MARIONETTES

In Polsky's windows twice each hour . . . you may see, enacted
for your holiday enjoyment . . . the Nativity. The original
Christmas scene, presented by the famed Kingsland Marionettes shows the three Wise men with their gifts of gold,
frankincense, and myrrh to the Christ Child. The Mother
Mary and Joseph may be seen, also. In what better way could
the true spirit of Christmas be portrayed than in the original scene from old Bethlehem. Bring the family to see the
Marionette Show in Polsky's Windows.

SEE and HEAR . . . Jolly Ol' Santa Claus
at the organ with his choir of angels singing
Christmas carols in Polsky's window at the corner of Main and State Streets.

*Plan to see all the Polsky windows Thanksgiv-
ing Day . . . enjoy the marionette show between
11 a. m. and 8:30 p. m. and plan, too, to shop
for everything under the Christmas tree at
Polsky's all season long.*

IN AKRON IT'S

Polsky's

November 24, 1948 newspaper ad for the Kingsland Marionettes' show in the Polsky's
window.

Throughout the 1950s, Polsky's re-installed the beautiful Star of Bethlehem window display in their north corner window. It was during this decade that the store began announcing that those who stopped to enjoy the traditional sacred window display could also hear Christmas carols now piped through speakers. One particular tune Polsky's promised to accompany the display was Ave Maria, a sacred and stirring song that complimented the dignified and reverent tone of the scene of the Nativity story.

In 1960, Polsky's updated their north corner sacred window with an imported, Italian-made Nativity display with ceramic figures. This set of ceramic sculptures was created by one of Italy's greatest ceramic artists, Professor Eugenio Pattarino, of Florence, Italy. The collection in Polsky's window was just one of six sets created by Pattarino and sold throughout the world. The exquisite Nativity statuary made by the Italian artist was known for its fine detailing and coloring. This particular ceramic display would be placed in the Polsky's window each Christmas throughout the rest of the 1960s. In a 2011 *Akron Beacon Journal* article, a testimonial claimed that the Polsky's Nativity set is currently displayed by the Sisters of Notre Dame-Chardon Province. While the Nativity set is undoubtedly similar to the one displayed at Polsky's—made by the same Italian maker—the sisters' records don't trace the set back to Polsky's.

O'Neil's department store also persuaded Akron's shoppers to patronize their store by means of a religious display. After a 1947 remodel of O'Neil's Main Street facade, the building now featured larger windows and a new marquee which served to keep rain, snow and wind away from those entering and exiting the store. In 1955, the top of the new marquee was used to display a Nativity scene. The extravagant Nativity set consisted of twenty three life-size, all-white figures depicting the traditional Bethlehem cast of characters including Mary, Joseph, baby Jesus, angels, the three magi and their camels, shepherds, sheep, and more. The grand and elegant collection was visible from across the street and even down the block.

Many people still remember the beautiful Nativity display

O'Neil's life-size Nativity set (detail) on display at Cornerstone Church at Portage Lakes in 2014. Photo: Dominic Caruso.

that stood on top of the marquee not only because of its size and dignity but because of the display's annual return to the same spot each year for decades. The sight of the Nativity display was awe-inspiring enough to be photographed for the front page of the local newspaper, *The Akron Beacon Journal* on Thanksgiving day, 1964.

While it is unclear which year was its last year downtown, it is clear that O'Neil's was still proud of the display and paid to advertise its presence and beauty in order to draw shoppers downtown through the 1970s. By the end of the 1980s, O'Neil's cherished life-size Nativity display was sold to a local congregation, Cornerstone Church, a Free Methodist Church at Portage Lakes, in whose care it still remains. Each year the church reinstalls the Nativity set on their property for the public to continue to enjoy.

HOW SANTA CAME TO TOWN

Over the years local retailers have developed the strategy of creating a special event to launch the official start of the Christmas shopping season. These special events have included times the curtains were pulled to reveal the annual Christmas window displays, the day when Archie the Snowman magically began to speak, when a store or indoor mall's elaborate Christmas attraction is finally open, and the circus-like spectacle of the arrival of Santa Claus to a store's location. These events illustrate the yearly competition between stores to attract attention and bring potential shoppers in the doors. The spectacle of Santa's arrival in special events all over town also reveals the escalating contest between downtown stores with the suburban shopping centers and eventually malls. Elsewhere in this book, I discuss the content of the downtown department stores' window displays, Archie the Snowman, and the area's breathtaking holiday attractions. But looking at the myriad of ways and the deluxe modes of transportation of Santa's arrival reveals how the rivalry between stores created an abundance of yuletide opportunities for Akron's children and adults to enjoy themselves.

1913 was a significant year in Akron's Christmas cultural history. It was the first year that a special event was created in a retail establishment in Akron to officially mark the start of the holiday shopping season. Coincidentally, both Yeager's and O'Neil's in 1913 publicized Santa's arrival in their toy departments as a special event, advertising both a time and a date for parents to bring their children down to the stores. These events were not just opportunities to visit with Santa Claus but to experience Santa's arrival at the store as an occasion worthy of special attention and notice. In 1913 a Yeager's ad announced, "Santa arrives in the Kiddie Paradise" at their store on the Friday after Thanksgiving at 10 a.m. in an automobile loaded down with toys. In the following day's newspaper, O'Neil's advertised the opening of Toyland as an event on the Friday after Thanksgiving, a day when schools were closed, and each child—accompanied by an adult—received a "pretty little xmas book" from Santa Claus in the store. Though it can be seen as early as 1913, the trend of creating a special event to kick off the start of the holiday season is still marked in Akron each year even now, in the twenty-first century.

DeWitt Motors' Alaskan Santa

The most outstanding Christmas attraction during the 1936 holiday season took place at a North Hill car dealership DeWitt Motors, located at 479 North Main Street, rather than a downtown department store. In December 1936, the car lot hosted the Hammond and Alaska Eskimo Troupe which featured an authentic North Pole-native Santa Claus. The personal appearance of the Inuk St. Nick also included free rides in a dog sled and sleigh, as well as live reindeer and husky sled dogs for the children to feed. The unique North Pole-inspired holiday attraction at DeWitt Motors was so popular and attracted such crowds that the event received a write-up in the *Beacon Journal*. The reporter pointed out that the Eskimo Santa even possessed black whiskers!

1953 was the beginning of a major shift in shopping for the residents of Akron. The city's first shopping plaza Wooster-Hawkins Plaza opened in Akron's southwest neighborhood. Instead of shoppers making a deliberate journey downtown to see what the major department stores stocked on their shelves for Christmas gifts, people could more easily drive (and find plenty of free parking) at a shopping center filled with smaller stores closer to

SANTA CLAUS COMES TO DeWITT'S

Boys and girls, mothers and fathers, here he is complete with his entire caravan of live reindeer, dog teams and sleighs

Don't Miss This Big Christmas Show At
DeWITT MOTORS, 479 N. MAIN ST.

TIME	FREE
ALL DAY WEDNESDAY, THURSDAY AND FRIDAY	TO EVERY CHILD ACCOMPANIED BY PARENTS A RIDE IN SANTA'S SLEIGH

December 2, 1936 newspaper ad for DeWitt Motors' Alaskan Christmas attraction.

home. Wooster-Hawkins Plaza signaled their entry in the competition for Christmas shoppers by creating a special event on the
Saturday after Thanksgiving, welcoming Santa Claus' arrival by
helicopter to the plaza's vast wide open parking lot. Just in case
that spectacle wasn't satisfying enough, the plaza also encouraged
everyone to "See the biggest Christmas tree in town!"

Not to be outdone, O'Neil's created a special event in 1954
welcoming the arrival of Santa Claus to their downtown department store by inviting children and their parents to watch St.
Nick fly in by helicopter and land on the top level of the store's
own parking deck. The spectacle was such a sight that O'Neil's
repeated the special event of Santa Claus arriving by helicopter in

Santa Claus

ARRIVES BY HELICOPTER THIS SATURDAY AT
WOOSTER-HAWKINS PLAZA

Shopping Center

PROMPTLY AT 2 P.M.

SEE THE BIGGEST CHRISTMAS TREE IN TOWN!

The party's at the Plaza! Bring the youngsters for their biggest thrill of the holiday season this week end! Santa Claus himself will swoop down out of the sky and land in the big Wooster-Hawkins Plaza parking lot. He'll leave the North Pole in time to arrive promptly at 2:00 Saturday afternoon, November 28. Don't miss his arrival by helicopter this weekend!

You'll not only see Santa Claus, but the biggest Christmas tree in town, complete with hundreds of sparkling, colorful lights! You'll find bargains galore in the stores at Wooster-Hawkins Plaza, too! Come join in the fun, and get acquainted with the money-saving advantages of one-stop Christmas shopping! Make out your list right now—and bring it along Saturday! The party's at the Plaza!

REMEMBER—SATURDAY AT 2 O'CLOCK!

PARKING AREA (REAR)	
WOOSTER-HAWKINS PLAZA	
PARKING AREA (FRONT)	
A HAWKINS AVENUE	

Plenty of
Free Parking
for
2,000 Cars

GUESS HOW MANY LIGHTS ON THE
GIANT CHRISTMAS TREE

And Win A TV Set ... A Wrist Watch ... A Bicycle

Pick up your nearest entry blank in any of the 17 Wooster-Hawkins Plaza stores. Then estimate the number of lights, sign your name and address and drop the blank in one of the special containers you'll find in each store. That's all there is to it. You may be a winner!

Christmas Carolers

Akron's leading choral groups will be at Wooster-Hawkins Plaza every Monday, Wednesday and Friday evening from December 7 to December 23, singing your favorite Christmas carols. Cast your vote for your favorite group when you come to the Plaza to shop. Two hundred dollars in cash awards will be made to the best carolers. If you belong to a singing group which would like to compete, get in touch with any Wooster-Hawkins Plaza Store Manager.

BIG HOLIDAY BARGAINS AT ALL THESE STORES

- ★ ACME SUPER MARKET
- ★ ALLEN CLEANERS
- ★ ARVALAN GIFTS
- ★ JONAS SHOPPES, INC.
- ★ JAMES HARDWARE
- ★ KROGER'S
- ★ LAWSON'S
- ★ McMULLEN JEWELRY
- ★ MOORE'S, INC.
- ★ NOBIL SHOE CO.
- ★ ROSEN'S BAKE SHOP
- ★ F. W. WOOLWORTH CO.

- ★ PEOPLES SERVICE DRUG STORES, INC.
- ★ WOOSTER-HAWKINS BEAUTY SALON
- ★ WOOSTER-HAWKINS BARBERSHOP
- ★ SKALL'S STORE FOR MEN

★ HAROLD'S RESTAURANT AND COCKTAIL LOUNGE

OPEN EVERY NIGHT, MONDAY THROUGH SATURDAY, TILL 9 P.M.

November 26, 1953 newspaper ad for Santa's arrival by helicopter at Wooster-Hawkins Plaza. This was the first instance of Santa arriving by helicopter in Akron.

1955 and '56, too. However, Santa's high-flying adventures had only just begun to enchant Akronites each Christmas. 1955 saw two additional events created welcoming Santa Claus by helicopter as well. The national chain store W. T. Grant Company sponsored a dramatic, must-see helicopter landing in downtown Barberton and at Fairlawn Plaza in 1955.

Across town in 1956, the new State Road Shopping Center in Cuyahoga Falls lured Christmas shoppers with a volley of fireworks to mark the beginning of the holiday shopping season. Children who came to see the fireworks also enjoyed free rocket rides in the parking lot. Santa Claus made an appearance, circulating throughout the plaza's thirty-three merchants to greet his many friends. This was the start of State Road Shopping Center's decades-old tradition of welcoming Santa and launching the holiday shopping season. For the next fifty years, State Road created many memorable Christmas special events including parades with the Cuyahoga Falls High School marching band and the tradition of Santa arriving by a fire truck with its sirens wailing and lights flashing.

To assert their dominance in the Christmas retail business, O'Neil's raised the stakes in the late 1950s. In 1957 Santa joined the space race when he arrived at O'Neil's front entrance escorted by the police and riding inside a gleaming, metal satellite! The spacecraft was described as Uncle Sam's satellite—not the pesky Russian's Sputnik which had crossed the sky earlier in October 1957. This must-see atomic age event was unforgettable.

The next year, in 1958, O'Neil's followed with a turn to the traditional by having their Santa Claus arrive by a sleigh pulled by reindeer. "…Weary of helicopters, satellites, and rockets—Santa's gone back to his original mode of transportation" read an ad for the 1958 special event that opened the start of the holiday shopping season at O'Neil's. And, O'Neil's kicked off the 1959 Christmas shopping season downtown with Santa Claus arriving at the store in a prairie schooner! "Santa's a hero in a ten-gallon hat arriving in a covered wagon…" says an ad promoting the event. This St. Nick donned boots, a vest, and a cowboy hat to the delight of children who were great fans of cowboy movies and TV shows in the 1950s.

November 21, 1957 newspaper ad for Santa's arrival at O'Neil's by "U.S. Santalite."

A western music band also played as this cowboy Santa came down Main Street waving to the crowds of eager children.

Almost too little too late, in 1961, Polsky's joined the fracas when they promoted their new parking deck on High Street. In a special event orchestrated on the Saturday before Thanksgiving, Polsky's welcomed the arrival of Santa Claus by helicopter, to the top of the new parking deck, inviting the public to enjoy the spectacle. The increasingly common "spectacle" of Santa arriving by helicopter was the one instance that the downtown retailer Polsky's attempted a unique arrival for their store Santa.

As more and more suburban shopping centers and plazas opened, they too wanted to draw potential shoppers. The decade of the 1960s saw an explosion of yuletide special events promoting Santa's arrival to various retail locations. Jolly St. Nick arrived by helicopter, riding atop a fire truck, by auto with a U. S. Marine military escort, accompanied by parades, clowns, free candy, and all sorts of discounts and sales all across town. These extravaganzas took place at nearly every retail complex in town at that time, including Arlington Plaza, Barberton's Magic City Shopping Center, Midway Plaza, Coventry Plaza, Lakemore Plaza, Akron Square Shopping Center, Norton Village, Wooster-Hawkins Plaza, South Plaza, and more. Throughout the 1960s, each year's events seemed to increase with intensity as Santa Claus arrived with more dramatic, breathtaking methods. For example, the chain discount store Maxam's drew attention in 1963 by having Santa Claus arrive by parachute to their location at Route 8 and 224.

Santa's high-flying arrival by helicopter peaked from 1964-68, when Akron's children could witness what could no longer be called a spectacle but an almost commonplace tradition. For example, in 1968, anyone could have seen Santa helicopter in to the parking lots at four different places at Christmas including Akron Square Plaza, Lakemore Plaza, State Road Shopping Center, and Arlington Plaza. Most of the other plazas welcomed Santa by parades, fire trucks, and other escorts—still a sight to behold, I'm sure.

The most original of the local Christmas special events to herald Santa's arrival started in 1967 at Chapel Hill Mall. For the mall's first official Christmas event, Santa arrived riding atop a live elephant! According to newspaper ads, the elephant was named Babe and she was the same elephant that actress Elizabeth Taylor rode during the filming of the 1954 movie *Elephant Walk*. After Santa rode into the mall's center court atop the elephant, the jolly fat man was established in his special chair to talk with all the children visitors the rest of the holiday season.

In 1968 the exotic journey was repeated and Santa Claus arrived at Chapel Hill Mall seated atop the elephant Babe. However this year, Babe was followed by a baby elephant named Tiny Tom. What a sight that must have been! In 1969, a newspaper ad for the special

November 23, 1967 newspaper ad for Santa's arrival at Chapel Hill Mall via Babe the elephant.

event read, "Day-After Thanksgiving tradition at Chapel Hill... Santa arriving in red velvet and gold splendor, astride the famous elephant from the circus and movie world, Babe. This year Baby Tom has learned a lot of neat tricks." Later another ad explained that the elephants Babe and Tom were from the exotic far away lands of Kokomo and Peru. I'm not a zoologist but I assume they meant the animals were bred there and not that the elephants were originally from these distant lands.

In 1971, the holiday special event with Santa and the elephants created a moment of unexpected excitement. A woman with a toddler in her arms stepped close to Babe to pet her trunk. Curious about her visitor, the elephant grabbed the box of shoes the woman had in her other hand. The frightened woman shrieked and the elephant's attendant came over and removed the box with the shoes from the animal's mouth! An *Akron Beacon Journal* photojournalist caught the hilarious moment on film for the front page of the newspaper.

The tradition of Santa arriving by elephant at Chapel Hill went on for nine years (1967-75.) During 1976 and '77, Chapel Hill Mall tested a new arrival means for their Santa Claus—they unveiled a Mystery Box in the mall's center concourse, promising to open the box in front of a live crowd on the day after Thanksgiving. I'm not sure this was much of a mystery for anyone over six years old, but it was original and it was fresh for Akron's kiddies. However, by 1978, Chapel Hill returned to welcoming Santa riding atop an elephant—a tradition that continued for another ten years (1978-87.)

By the mid-80s, Chapel Hill had found another animal supplier for their annual Christmas event. In 1985, the Asian elephant named Jack, from Bobby Moore's Performing Elephants in Michigan, carried Santa Claus to the center of the mall and offered rides to several children of local merchants afterwards. However, by 1988, Santa's arrival riding an elephant was no more and the almost twenty year tradition was put to rest for good. During the kick-off event at the mall in 1988, Santa arrived at Chapel Hill in a horse drawn sleigh. Parades with balloons, marching bands, clowns, and costumed characters replaced the annual elephant rides. The age of Christmas extravagance to mark the annual start of the holiday shopping season was mostly in the past.

During the twenty years that Santa arrived at the mall by means of an elephant, other spectacular events around Akron were also being generated. Santa continued to arrive at several retail destinations each year by helicopter. In addition, in 1970, Santa skydived into the parking lot at Summit Mall to dazzle and amaze the gathered crowds. This same stunt had been performed in 1963 in South Akron, but it was still undoubtably a breathtaking sight, several years later. In 1976 and '77, Summit Mall felt the pinch in business from the new mall across town, Rolling Acres. For both of those years at the holidays, Summit Mall welcomed their mall Santa Claus' arrival by "Santa-copter" as well.

In 1975, the newly opened Rolling Acres took full advantage of the *Akron Beacon Journal's* advertising pages to alert residents of the special event happening at the mall. Rolling Acres' first holiday season included a grand welcome for the mall's Santa Claus by having him lead the "Fantasia of all Christmas parades." Santa was joined by Mrs. Claus, and Tommy the Clown from the Ringling Brothers/Barnum and Bailey Circus, along with several other performers who escorted him to his Snow Bird House located in the North Court of the mall where children visited him with their Christmas wishes. The clowns and performers from the internationally-renowned circus entertained children and shoppers after the parade and at twenty-minute intervals throughout the day.

By the 1980s, each of the annual special events that launched the start of the holiday shopping season became less about breathtaking stunts and more about creating an elaborate party atmosphere. Ultimately, it was and continues to be about bringing people to the retail location and igniting the holiday spirit. After the downtown stores closed for good and the malls were the area's dominant shopping locations, fewer efforts were made and smaller events were planned for shoppers who required less motivation— the era of tremendous competition between retail spaces was largely in the past.

To adapt to changing consumer habits, by the 1980s more and more of the Christmas events for families were scheduled for weekday evenings at the malls—instead of the Friday or Saturday after Thanksgiving. This new trend for Christmas attractions reflected an effort to accommodate working parents' schedules. The late '80s also saw another popular attraction at Rolling Acres. The theme "A Jingle Bell Christmas" was repeated for several years at Rolling Acres and for Santa's arrival, two hundred children received free jingle bells to ring in the start of the holiday shopping season each year.

Although special events to mark the start of the gift-giving season continued throughout Akron area, one of the last significant events occurred at nearby Belden Village Mall in 1988. Belden Village welcomed their mall's Santa with special fanfare, televising the event on the morning TV show *AM Cleveland* with an appearance by the popular show's host Scott Newell. Now area shoppers didn't even need to leave their homes to witness this once-a-year special Christmas event.

In 1989, Summit Mall welcomed their mall Santa along with performances from the cast of a musical production of *The Wizard of Oz* from the Carousel Dinner Theatre. Also in 1989, Rolling Acres Mall repeated their Jingle Bell Christmas promotion and invited the Akron Youth Symphony, with conductor Keith Lockhart, to perform. Yes, you read that correctly, I mean the same Keith Lockhart that briefly conducted the Cleveland Orchestra and has since gone on to become the conductor for the prestigious Boston Pops Orchestra as well as the BBC Concert Orchestra. In 1994, Rolling Acres created another splash for St. Nick with the event "Santa's Starlight Arrival" which included the Akron Youth Symphony, and performances by Karen Gabay and Raynard Rodriguez of the Cleveland Ballet Company and the Cuyahoga Valley Youth Ballet. Did you know Gabay and Rodriguez appeared in the second season of ABC's *Dancing with the Stars* TV series? Even if these events were some of the last hurrahs of Akron's special events at the malls at Christmas time, they were indeed some of the finest.

November 17, 1994 newspaper ad for Rolling Acres Mall's Starlight Arrival of Santa.

If you're wondering where these special events have gone and why they have largely disappeared, it's because we have allowed them to be replaced by Black Friday promises of deep discount sales. Consumers no longer require entertainment or special attractions for their children but prefer to stand in long lines to shop. It should be noted that in downtown Akron, there remains a Welcome Santa Parade each year that rolls down Main Street on the Saturday after Thanksgiving. This tradition has been going on since 1987 and continues each year. However, the fanfare of the downtown Santa parade isn't sponsored by a retail establishment with the intention to entertain and draw shoppers since there are no more department stores on Main Street, and very few retailers downtown anymore. The annual parade is instead a civic, public event for families to mark the start of the holidays.

Downtown Parades

Every year Akronites enjoy the Welcome Santa parade that marches down Main Street through downtown. An annual tradition since 1987, the Welcome Santa parade features costumed characters, local social organizations, bands, vintage cars, and of course, Santa himself. However long before this holiday fixture, Main Street saw some pretty memorable holiday parades.

The headline "Santa Claus is Coming to Akron" dominated the *Akron Times-Press* front pages in 1926 in anticipation of that year's Christmas parade. In addition to the headlines, the sponsoring newspaper filled its front pages in the weeks leading up to the December event with details on Santa's journey from the North Pole to Akron. The build-up to the parade was made even more exciting because Santa was bringing an exotic special guest with him. Santa was to be accompanied by an Eskimo family consisting of Tautuk, his wife Mrs. Tautuk, their two children Billy and Mary, and six live reindeer.

On Monday, December 13th, 1926 the daytime parade was scheduled for 2:30 p.m. so the local schools were dismissed early. The parade's grand marshal was I. M. Myers and the master of ceremonies was C. W. Seiberling, two of Akron's most prominent businessmen. The parade included fairy tale-themed floats with Goldilocks and the Three Bears, and The Old Woman Who Lives in a Shoe with costumed characters. There was also an igloo float and one decorated with Santa's toy shop. Five Akron area high school bands performed as well as Santa's band, and a synthetic

Get Set! Here's Where To See Big Yule Parade!

November 24, 1937 *Akron Beacon Journal* Christmas Parade route through downtown Akron.

snowstorm. According to the newspaper's coverage the day after the event, it was estimated that two hundred thousand people attended the daytime parade. Crowds pressed onto the sidewalks and spilled into the streets. There were so many people that filled the streets that transportation into downtown and away from it was paralyzed for hours.

Little more than a decade later, Akron saw its next holiday parade. In 1937, the Christmas Parade was sponsored by the *Akron Beacon Journal* and was held downtown on Main Street, the day after Thanksgiving. Hoping to draw in the shoppers from the crowds of parade watchers, nearly every store downtown advertised special attractions in their stores to kick off the start of the Christmas shopping season.

In addition to parade floats, costumed characters, and marching bands, the 1937 Christmas parade promised forty oversized, inflated balloons to amaze the crowds. Among them were Mickey Mouse, Donald Duck, a giant clown, Elmer Elephant, Harry Hippopotamus, Krazy Katz, Dracula Dragon, and twelve-foot-high inflated letters that spelled out Merry Christmas. These balloons were the same type that walked the Macy's Thanksgiving Parade each year. Perhaps some of the balloons were the same ones used in New York since Akron's own Goodyear manufactured the balloons for both parades.

Despite the intermittent rain on Friday November 26, 1937, the well-advertised parade downtown ended up drawing too many people. It was later described in the newspaper almost as a disaster. Estimating that 175,000 or more people showed up (the total population of Akron at that time was about 250,000), the width of the streets to the store fronts couldn't accommodate the crowds! The parade itself moved at a snail's pace as the police had to clear the streets a few dozen feet at a time, asking parade viewers to move back and clear the path for the parade to be able to move forward. It was described that parade viewers were hanging out of Main Street building windows and on rooftops to catch a glimpse of the Christmas parade that included more than a dozen local bands, oversized inflated balloons, and the man of the hour, Santa Claus. The wait to see Santa was well worth it—Santa arrived, seated in an airplane cockpit that taxied down Main Street!

Another memorable parade occurred in 1955. Akron's Chamber of Commerce and the Akron Merchants Association organized the Thanksgiving Day Parade to help encourage area shoppers to make the trip downtown for Christmas. Sixteen floats manned by area high school students were joined by numerous high school marching bands, and costumed characters—including characters from the *Wizard of Oz*. The holiday parade circled the downtown business district, from Grant Street to Exchange, to Main Street, to Market Street, to Broadway, left on Center Street, and returning to Grant Street. I can imagine what a happy spectacle this must have been. Of course, both O'Neil's and Polsky's elaborate fantasy window displays were already unveiled by the start of the parade on Thanksgiving Day. In 1955, Polsky's not only repeated their reverent Nativity display in one window but they also filled a series of windows with the story from the popular poem "The Night Before Christmas" by Clement C. Moore. Across the street, O'Neil's windows featured a fantasy display of forest animals preparing for Christmas. When was the last time you visited downtown Akron to watch a holiday parade?

NOW APPEARING:
SANTA'S CELEBRITY GUESTS

What do stores do when all their competitors offer the same, or nearly the same, shopping experience? This was a common problem faced by Akron retailers over the decades. When nearly every store puts out an eye-catching toy display in their toy departments and employs a Santa Claus to greet each child, what more can be done to bring patrons into the store to spend their holiday money? One strategy has been to create a special event—a temporary offer with overwhelming appeal to drive people to a particular location. Celebrity appearances make successful Christmas special events, and have most often been used to bring shoppers into the stores on the Friday or Saturday after Thanksgiving.

Some celebrity appearances in Akron stores at Christmas time were people or characters on promotional tours around the country. Many other celebrity appearances were from children's entertainment, and eventually television. Still other appearances, such as beauty pageant winners and sports stars, were clearly intended to also lure adults. According to the newspaper advertising that preceded these special events, the celebrities most often brought photographs of themselves, signed autographs, and many times they handed out free candy. It should be noted that celebrities never replaced Santa Claus at these events. Instead the appearances by celebrities usually enhanced the special events where St. Nick made his own debut. Retailers knew that the longer visitors stayed inside the store, the more likely they were to make a purchase.

A monopoly on celebrities with white beards: November 29, 1917 newspaper ad for Uncle Sam's and Santa's joint appearance at the M. O'Neil Company.

Almost one hundred years ago in Akron, the M. O'Neil Company created one of the first and certainly the most patriotic celebrity appearances. In 1917, filled with flag-waving support for the American soldiers heading to the conflict in Europe, O'Neil's created a Christmas attraction that would never be duplicated. In their store downtown, they encouraged children to not only share their Christmas wish with Santa Claus but also come and greet Uncle Sam. The image of Uncle Sam was a popular one, seen in enlistment posters during World War I. If I had been a kid in 1917, I know I would not have missed the opportunity to shake hands with everyone's favorite icon of America.

In 1928 during the holiday season, the downtown retailer Bear Furniture Company placed a most unusual sight in their front windows. Automa, the Human Automaton, entertained and delighted everyone who passed by Bear's window. "Is he alive?" the store ad begs readers to investigate. The robot-like moving creature was also a cross-promotion for the screening of a silent Lon Chaney movie, *West of Zanzibar,* by noted director Tod Browning, playing at The Strand movie house across town. The Bear Furniture Co. ad promised, "…a season pass to The Strand Theater given to the person making the human automaton laugh or smile."

During the first week of December in 1931, Yeager's department store featured a similar attraction, another robot-man. "Westinghouse Electrical Show presents Willie Vocalite" an unsettling, "electrical man of the age," which was an actual 3-D robot that responded to sound commands. Although the robot seems crude by today's standards of electronics, this well-known mechanism was a very early advancement in robot technology. The ad claimed, "the robot responds to the will of the operator as the requests penetrate his intricate electrical brain." There were four performances daily of the robot-man who lit a cigarette, smoked it, turned on any electrical appliance (Westinghouse, undoubtedly), shot a gun, and other things. The sight of Willie on Yeager's second floor was so entertaining that the *Akron Beacon Journal* ran a follow-up story after the electric robot's debut.

Across Main Street in 1932, O'Neil's eschewed the mechanical and hosted a special animal act, the world-famous dog, Silver King, for an in-store appearance. The popular and talented German Shepherd was a trained dog that made many personal appearances and gave safety tips for children. Silver King went on to make several appearances in movies, including 1933's *Rusty Rides Again*

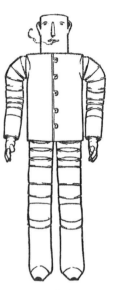
December 7, 1931 newspaper ad for Willie Vocalite's appearance at Yeager's.

and 1938's *On the Great White Trail.* At O'Neil's, the canine appeared in the store's second floor auditorium, and autographed—with his own paw—copies of a Silver King storybook, penned by W. F. Malloy, for everyone who attended the special event. Silver King's owner and trainer Arthur Butler was also present.

In the post-war era of the 1950s, the economy and population in Akron had expanded and we experienced the beginning of the golden era of Christmas window displays, led by retail competitors Polsky's and O'Neil's downtown. This meant that when the shopping plazas—and eventually the malls—opened in the greater-Akron area, they needed to create even more impressive special events on the weekend after Thanksgiving each year in order to draw people to their new locations. Many of these special events included celebrity appearances.

For example, in 1955, the Cuyahoga Falls' Front Street merchants association planned a holiday event which welcomed children to meet Santa Claus and the well-known local TV celebrity Uncle Jake from *Uncle Jake's House*. Uncle Jake, played by Gene Carroll (yes—the same Gene Carroll that would later host the talent show) on WEWS-TV aired from Cleveland. The after school TV series *Uncle Jake's House* which began in 1948 was the first locally produced kiddie program in Cleveland and one of the earliest in the country.

During the following holiday season, the Front Street merchants in Cuyahoga Falls organized a tree lighting event welcoming Santa Claus to greet each child in attendance. The event also included the local children's TV celebrity Captain Penny, from Cleveland's own WEWS-TV. The railroad engineer, Captain Penny, was the host of *Captain Penny's Fun House* played by actor Ron Penfound. His local TV series began in 1955 and aired weekday afternoons and eventually on Saturday mornings as well. Captain Penny engaged young viewers with advice on politeness, manners, and respect during segments between cartoons and comedic short films.

And, at Christmas the next year, the Cuyahoga Falls Front Street merchants once again hosted another special celebrity appearance to bolster the debut of Santa Claus. In 1957, children were greeted by kiddie TV host Barnaby. Barnaby, played by Linn Sheldon, first went on the air in Cleveland in 1957 on KYW—which eventually became WKYC-TV. Barnaby was a charming elf in a suit jacket and straw hat that introduced cartoons. Attesting to his good-natured charm, Barnaby eventually was the longest running kiddie TV host in Cleveland, staying on the air until 1990.

Attempting to compete with the expanding numbers of celebrity appearances in stores, the downtown retailer Yeager's department store hosted their own celebrity during their kick-off Santa Claus event in 1958. For one day only, Yeager's store proudly welcomed children to meet their store Santa and Miss Barbara, the TV host of Cleveland's own *Romper Room* TV program. Barbara

Plummer worked as Miss Barbara at WEWS-TV's daily *Romper Room* series from 1958 through 1971. Does anyone remember if Miss Barbara brought her magic mirror to Yeager's at Christmas time in 1958?

South of Akron's downtown, a new collection of stores had recently opened called Arlington Plaza. During the holidays in 1958, Arlington Plaza attracted attention by bringing in Kookie the Clown, a Detroit television star and radio personality. Kookie made a three-day personal appearance at the plaza handing out free balloons—and judging from the photos of Kookie in the newspaper ads—scaring the living daylights out of children. In 1960, another clown dominated Christmas. At Akron's east side Lakemore Plaza children greeted not just Santa Claus, but Bozo the Clown, the WJW-TV star.

As more shopping centers and plazas were opening up all over greater-Akron, special celebrities continued to be hired to enhance the official start of the holiday shopping season. In 1962 at Barberton's Magic City Shopping Center, TV celebrity Woodrow made an appearance the same day Santa Claus arrived. Woodrow the Woodsman was a character brought to life by actor Clay Conroy on the TV series *Barnaby* in 1960. Barnaby and Woodrow enter-tained children from The Enchanted Forest on TV, talking with animals by the wishing well. Eventually the popular woodsman got his own Saturday morning show *Woodrow's Zoo Parade*. Woodrow had a very distinctive appearance as a woodsman with a choppy uneven haircut and a furry mustache. Newspaper ads promised that Woodrow would wear his famous make-up and costume to the Christmas event.

Across town in 1962, the local discount store Clarkins also arranged in-store appearances of two celebrity guests to promote the Christmas shopping season. At the Clarkins in Kent, children collected the autograph of Miss Barbara from *Romper Room*. And at the Clarkins store on Hawkins Avenue in Akron, children visited with TV show host Captain Penny.

One of the more exciting, and perhaps the most outstanding celebrity appearance happened during the 1963 holiday season. The

November 21, 1963 newspaper ad for Ghoulardi's scheduled appearance in downtown Barberton, Ohio.

merchants in downtown Barberton invited children to meet Santa Claus and none other than the irreverent Cleveland TV horror movie host Ghoulardi. This celebrity event took place during the peak of Ghoulardi's popularity, and was scheduled months in advance. Unfortunately, it coincided with the tragic events occurring in Dallas at that time. The Ghoulardi appearance was scheduled to take place in the morning on Saturday, November 23, the day after President Kennedy was assassinated. Though all the downtown Akron stores, schools and most businesses would close on Monday, November 25 as a day of mourning, it is not clear whether the Ghoulardi holiday event was cancelled or indeed went on as scheduled.

The peak of celebrity appearances to help launch the start of the holiday shopping season in Akron was 1964. In just one weekend, children could get autographs from five different celebrities at multiple events. In downtown, Polsky's toyland hosted Akron's own WAKR-TV children's host Professor Jack. Jack Bennett played the scholarly TV host on the daily TV program from 1963-66.

(Interestingly, Bennett created the Professor Jack children's character while working at O'Neil's Georgian Room restaurant during Christmas years before!) Like many of the local TV programs created for children at that time, Professor Jack performed skits between cartoons.

Across town in 1964, the shopping plazas lured shoppers with celebrity appearances as well. Wooster-Hawkins Plaza brought in Santa Claus for the kiddies and an appearance with the reigning Miss U.S.A., Jeanne Marie Quinn from East Meadow, New York. In 1964, the blonde, blue-eyed, beauty pageant winner was a mathematics student at Hofstra University, and the promise of her autographed photo surely appealed to adults as well. In 1964, the local discount store Clarkins arranged celebrity appearances by Captain Penny and *Romper Room's* Miss Barbara, for a second year in a row. And, Barberton's Magic City Shopping Center welcomed TV host Woodrow for the kiddies and another appearance of the beauty pageant winner, Miss U.S.A. Jeanne Marie Quinn, to lure adults as well.

When the malls began opening in Akron, they also invited celebrities to draw attention to their holiday events. In 1965, for the first Christmas season at the new Summit Mall, young tots welcomed Santa Claus and the television celebrity, Franz the Toymaker. Ray Stawiarski created the character of Franz and appeared on Cleveland's WJW-TV starting in 1962. The popular TV host was a toy maker that spoke with a German accent and helped children to build their own playthings.

In 1966, Chapel Hill mall opened. The mall's Christmas attractions didn't begin until the following year, and the start of the holiday season in 1966 only a few of the individual stores in the mall were open for business. Still, a few of the stores hosted their own holiday promotional events. The men's store Koch's brought in the Cleveland Browns players Leroy Kelly and quarterback Frank Ryan. Kelly was voted into the Professional Football Hall of Fame in 1994 and Ryan is remembered as being one of the more outstanding quarterbacks in Browns history.

The following year, in 1967, Summit Mall welcomed TV show

December 7, 1967 newspaper ad for "Franz" the Toymaker's appearance at Arlington Plaza.

host Captain Penny to sign autographs and to greet children during the start of the holiday season. And, in 1968, Arlington Plaza welcomed the popular children's TV star Franz the Toymaker from WJW-TV for an afternoon to hand out free candy and photos.

In 1970, at the city's center, the downtown retailers association developed its own Christmas time activities to give families more incentive to return to downtown to shop for the holidays. The new Cascade ice skating rink welcomed noted figure skaters Hayes Alan Jenkins and his wife Carol Heiss Jenkins for a skating demonstration. Jenkins won the gold medal in the 1956 Winter Olympics and his wife won the silver medal at the 1956 Olympics and the gold at the 1960 Olympics. The celebrity couple, then living in the Akron area, also flipped the switch on the Christmas light displays downtown in a special ceremony.

With the height of competition between stores at Christmas time in Akron over, spending money to organize special events was largely unnecessary. However, a few special events still occurred. In 1976, Halle's store at Summit Mall hosted a *Mr. Jingeling's Musical Show*—a special production presented on two consecutive Wednesday evenings in December 1976 to entertain children. Additionally, parents could purchase Mr. Jingeling gift wrap to decorate Christmas gifts under the tree at home. The popular Mr. Jingeling was known as one of Santa's helpers who kept track of the keys at the North Pole, and was a unique promotional character from Halle's department store in Cleveland. Akron children may have been familiar with Mr. Jingeling because he appeared on the TV series Captain Penny for many years each

Christmas season. However, the Christmas character was known for his yearly appearances in Cleveland's Halle's store during the 1950s and '60s, and didn't make an appearance in Akron until after the height of his fame had mostly passed. Mr. Jingeling's appearance at Summit Mall may have appealed to the nostalgia of adults in 1976 but would have missed the attention of most TV viewing youngsters in Akron at that time. And in 1977 Rolling Acres brought in the famous magician Harry Albacker to perform at selected intervals. Albacker was an entertainer of much acclaim and even performed at the White House dozens of times during the Roosevelt, Eisenhower, Kennedy, Nixon, and Carter administrations. In 1977, Albacker's magic show was only part of the Rolling Acres' breathtaking Christmas attraction, Disney's Magic Kingdom, which included an elaborate Disney display and costumed characters. The world-famous magician and the Disney Magic Kingdom Christmas display was repeated the following year as well.

CHRISTMAS MONKEY BUSINESS: ORGAN GRINDERS

Of the many attractions and special guests brought in to entertain and amuse shoppers at Christmas time in downtown Akron, an organ grinder accompanied by a trained monkey was a long-standing favorite at Polsky's.

In the 1930s and into the '40s, the Old World organ grinder Dominic and his monkey Julia performed for the young and old alike at Polsky's each year at Christmas. Their appearance at the opening of the store's toyland helped to make the after-Thanksgiving event one not to be missed. In case you don't know, an organ grinder is a performer who carries a mobile musical instrument. Usually, he plays a series a tunes and collects coins from spectators while his pet monkey performs tricks for the crowd that gathers around to watch and listen to the music.

An *Akron Times-Press* newspaper article, from November 28th, 1936, provided a profile of Polsky's organ grinder Dominic Fundino from Cleveland. The resident of Little Italy was born in Rome in 1878. After coming to America, he saved his money to buy a barrel organ and a monkey, and had worked for forty-five years at his trade, becoming a father and grandfather in that time. Julia, his third monkey, was a capuchin from South America. Dominic said he began to train Julia when she was just a few months old with small morsels of food and a bit of kindness. Eventually she was able to perform six tricks, including tossing her cap into the air and catching it, waving a tiny baton to the music, performing a slow

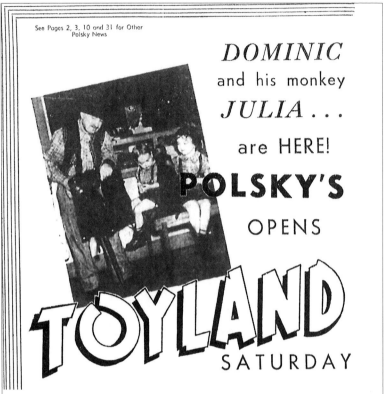

See Pages 2, 3, 10 and 31 for Other Polsky News

DOMINIC

and his monkey

JULIA . . .

are HERE!

POLSKY'S

OPENS

TOYLAND

SATURDAY

November 18, 1938 newspaper ad for Dominic the Organ Grinder & his monkey Julia at Polsky's.

dance, playing cymbals, smoking a pipe, and carrying a small cup from patron to patron to collect coins. She would also take children's hands if they reached out to her. Dominic preferred working at the downtown department stores at Christmas because working outdoors made his monkey more susceptible to pneumonia—which had killed two previous monkeys. Dominic and Julia were a popular attraction throughout northeast Ohio and performed at the Great Lakes Exposition in 1936 and the New York World's Fair in 1939.

Starting in the 1960s, Polsky's once again employed an organ grinder and his monkey to entertain in the store at Christmas time. Returning to this quaint form of entertainment was certainly a way to tap into Akron residents' feelings of nostalgia for the decades earlier when they welcomed Dominic and Julia at Christmas time. In the 1960s, Polsky's hosted a man named Tony to play his Old World hurdy gurdy machine and entertain with his pet monkey. Adults who grew up in the 1930s and '40s were now able to bring their children (and maybe even grandchildren) to experience entertainment they had enjoyed at Polsky's in the past. Tony and his monkey returned to Polsky's each Christmas throughout the 1960s. In the early 1970s, Tony made visits not only at the downtown Polsky's store during the holidays but also to many of the branch locations too.

WINTER WONDERLANDS: IN-STORE ATTRACTIONS & WALK-THROUGHS

Since the turn of the twentieth century, Akron retailers have depended on the sales made during the Christmas holiday season for a large part of their annual revenue. One way that retailers have tried to stand out from their competitors is by creating a holiday attraction, or a unique lure to pull potential shoppers in to the store. When every store in Akron's shopping district had their own Santa Claus, retailers began creating once-a-year special events to welcome Santa. When every store offered to sell toys, retailers began designing Toyland Christmas displays to outshine their competitors. And, when retailers in Akron welcomed clowns, trained animal acts, and celebrity guests to entertain potential shoppers, an escalation in Christmas attractions popped up all over town to keep up with the competition. Yes, Archie the Talking Snowman was a Christmas attraction created by Chapel Hill Mall to bring in potential shoppers. All of the local, major retailers in Akron created Christmas attractions. It's interesting to see the history of how the in-store attractions developed around town and witness the competition between the retailers. The breathtaking and amazing Christmas attractions created by the downtown department stores reveal the level of competition over money spent by the residents of the Rubber Capital of the World. It all went towards the evolution of an exciting Christmas culture that could have only existed here in Akron.

There existed an exciting time in the 1930s and '40s in Akron

Opening of
TOYLAND Saturday,
10:00 A. M.

COME!

Hurra! OLD SANTA CLAUS

Is Back at Yeager's

After a whole year's absence Santa Claus is back and has established
his headquarters on the

THIRD FLOOR

And Will Open

Bring the
Children
Tomorrow

TOYLAND

To All Girls and Boys

TOYS

Third Floor

TOMORROW

You Are Invited

New Features!　　*New Fun!*　　*New Thrills!*

In This Wonderland of TOYS

Bring all the Children
Tomorrow

The Yeager Toy Store is a veritable emporium of all the toys that Santa
Claus has had time to make since last Christmas.

To Children Visiting
TOYLAND
accompanied by parents, we will give a
Canary Bird Whistle **FREE**.
Also instructed how to use them.
We have only 1,000 whistles, so be
bright and early

The C·H·Yeager company

November 26, 1915 newspaper ad for Yeager's Toyland display.

when the downtown department stores were creating and inventing Christmas attractions to outshine each other. By the 1950s and '60s, Christmas attractions were dominated by talking characters and the arrival of Santa Claus became an extraordinary special event. This was during the golden age of downtown window displays. By the 1970s and '80s, Christmas attractions became more competitive between the area's malls and plazas, while the remaining downtown department stores created a few extra special attractions in their last desperate attempts to stay in business.

At the turn of the twentieth century, retail stores in downtown Akron were filled with the Christmas spirit. Storefront windows were filled with decorations and merchandise for Christmas gift giving. Many retailers ordered larger supplies of toys, dolls, and specialty children's items months in advance and they displayed this merchandise in temporarily expanded areas of the store, referred to as toyland. Most stores used language like Toyland, Toytown, Jack Frost Land etc., to describe the specially decorated expanded toy departments. This choice of wording was used to add wonderment and amusement to the shopping experience. The week after Thanksgiving in 1910, both the C. H. Yeager Company and the M. O'Neil Company, among numerous other stores, placed ads promoting their children's toylands. The Yeager's ad even explained that they removed the carpets and rugs department to make room for the expanded children's toy display. The toylands also featured "toy exhibits" or large displays of the toys available for purchase in the store where children could see the toys, touch them, or even witness a demonstration of the toys' functions.

1912 was a special year for O'Neil's because they not only had Santa Claus in the store handing out fairy tale books to the kiddies, but they also brought in a representative from the Bing Factory, in Nuremberg, Germany, to show off and demonstrate the wide variety of toys his factory made—including toy engines, cars, walking dogs, and other toys. Not to be outdone, that same year the downtown retailers Yeager's, Federman's, Akron Dry Goods, Home Furniture Company, Central Hardware and Stove Company, Kirk Company, and even the shoe store Lloyd's, advertised their toylands—many of which also included the opportunity for children to greet Santa Claus in the store.

In 1914, the bloody conflict in Europe dominated the daily front pages of the *Akron Beacon Journal*. This year, O'Neil's responded to the previous year's competition over holiday shoppers by inviting them to toyland to visit Santa Claus—who waited for visitors in

"Merry Old Santa Claus"

is in Toyland at the M O'Neil Co. this week. He is giving a nice little book of Fairy Tales to the little boys and girls who come with their parents.

All the way from the Bing factory in Naumberg, Germany, a man has come to show the wonderful engines, cars, walking dogs and other things this week.

The opening of Toyland last week was a big success and so many dolls and toys were bought that we want to remind you of getting your share early. It will save time later and we will reserve them for you now for a small deposit.

December 2, 1912 newspaper ad for the M. O'Neil Co. Toyland & visits from Santa & a Bing factory toy employee.

his own elaborate display. "Bring the little folks to meet Santa in his log cabin home and get a little gift from him," read one O'Neil's ad of the time. Visitors were encouraged to see Santa's workshop and log cabin home. The creation of elaborately decorated, themed displays to surround where Santa Claus greeted his visitors was another trend that would continue in Akron until the end of the twentieth century.

The next significant step in creating Christmas attractions occurred in 1928. O'Neil's newly built store on Main Street also included a new auditorium on the second floor. Here, store employees established The Enchanted Forest, a fantasy exhibit with elves, fairies, animals of the forest, and more, as a walk-through wonderland display for visitors to experience on their way to greet Santa Claus. The store's commitment to their first in-store Christmas display can be seen in the unique way they promoted the experience. The store ran a serialized adventure story in the *Akron Beacon Journal* and the *Akron Times-Press* over several weeks.

The ENCHANTED FOREST in O'NEIL'S AUDITORIUM

Akron's little folks will be enraptured with this lovely Land of Make Believe, where the Enchanted Forest is all a-glitter with brilliantly lighted scenes from the best loved Fairy Tales.

For a long time we dreamed of the first Christmas display in our new store. As a result here's this wonderful surprise in store for you.

WE BELIEVE THAT NO CHRISTMAS DISPLAY IN AMERICA HAS EVER EXCEEDED THIS. It took time, it took money, but WE FELT THAT NOTHING WAS TOO GOOD FOR THE KIDDIES. And now we are assured that you will long remember their delight as one of the keenest pleasures of the Holiday season.

THEN, RIGHT IN THE CENTER OF THE ENCHANTED FOREST IS TOYLAND, just loaded with toys and games -- endless in number -- a most unique display -- one of the most wonderful ever assembled. Dolls and toys that will not only fascinate the kiddies, but Fathers and Mothers, and Aunts and Uncles, too.

And there are -- Oh, Well! Words simply can't tell you the story of this breath-taking exhibition. IT MUST BE SEEN TO BE APPRECIATED. It's a real Christmas surprise that will not only enrapture the children, but will appeal to the youth that's in the heart of each and every grown-up.

THE M.O'NEIL CO.
AKRON'S GREATEST STORE
O'Neil's Regular Store News Page 18

November 16, 1928 newspaper ad for O'Neil's "Enchanted Forest" walk-through and serialized adventure story featuring the characters Bob and Betty.

This clever form of advertising not only sparked the imagination of young folks but appealed to the child inside adults as well. In 1929, O'Neil's once again used their second floor auditorium for a Christmas display—this year drawing potential shoppers into the store with a lively circus theme. To draw in more visitors, the store hired a clown and a circus barker to entertain the hundreds of children that visited. The clown and barker were positioned at the head of the escalator on the second floor to direct shoppers to the circus display and the toyland.

The following years would see more competition for O'Neil's from its retail peers. In 1931, with their newly expanded building dedicated, Yeager's rolled out the red carpet to its Christmas shoppers by welcoming them to greet the store Santa Claus and meet a circus clown named Zero. Zero, who appeared in the Sparks Circus and the Hagenbeck-Wallace Circus, ushered the store's visitors to the newly expanded toyland. In 1932, Polsky's hosted their very first Christmas attraction, the Pamahasika's Society Circus animal show. The acts included trained dogs, wonder ponies, performing clown monkeys Bozo and Oswald, and a bird circus. The ads claimed the bird show consisted of forty live birds performing tricks. The trained bird acts included Billy the Mathematical Wizard, birds that waltzed, a mother bird that pushed her baby bird in a carriage, birds that rode a Ferris wheel, birds that put out a fire, and birds that fought a battle. A required ten cent admission fee to see the trained animal acts was collected and donated to a local children's charity. Also in 1932, O'Neil's entertained their patrons with special celebrity guest, the trained dog Silver King.

In 1933, a landmark in Christmas attractions was created. O'Neil's upped the ante to compete for Akron's attention when it created an all-new walk-through experience on its second floor. For twenty-five cents, children "rode" to the North Pole by means of a zeppelin. A giant, metal structure allowed children to walk through the aircraft. It featured cabin windows through which they could follow the zeppelin's journey past fairy castles, Eskimo villages, and passing aircraft. Exiting at the other end of the zeppelin, the children arrived at the fairyland of the North Pole, otherwise known as O'Neil's toyland. This unique Christmas attraction was not only a once-in-a-lifetime experience for the children in 1933 but the heartbreak of every Akron child ever since. The walk-through zeppelin "ride" at O'Neil's was such an amazing sight to behold, the local newspaper wrote a follow-up story after

In Akron's Largest Most Complete TOYLAND
Friday --- The Command Will Be

"UP SHIP"
In O'NEIL'S TOYLAND
ZEPPELIN

- *You've Seen Them Built*
- *You've Seen Them Launched*
- *You've Seen Them Flying*

Now Boys and Girls You Can Enjoy a Thrilling Sky Ride in
O'NEIL'S TOYLAND ZEPPELIN

25c a Ride

and when your journey is finished you will receive a surprise
Christmas Package.

Toyland is open. The Zeppelin will make flights each day from now until
Christmas Eve. Every boy and girl in Akron will want to ride in this new
Zeppelin.

Toyland—Second Floor

The M. O'NEIL Co.

AKRON'S GREATEST STORE

November 16, 1933 newspaper ad for O'Neil's "Zeppelin" walk-through.

the rigid airship's debut and included photos (and free publicity)
for the O'Neil's attraction.

The zeppelin Christmas attraction at O'Neil's was made even
more meaningful for Rubber City residents because Akron was
the location where Goodyear manufactured both rigid aircraft
(zeppelins), and non-rigid airships known as blimps. The O'Neil's

zeppelin "ride" may have been more thrilling than some may have wanted because the rigid airship the USS Akron experienced a deadly crash earlier that year, in April 1933. And you thought Archie was scary!

The following year, in 1934, O'Neil's constructed another unforgettable Christmas attraction. O'Neil's second floor toyland featured Walt Disney's cartoon icon in a Mickey Mouse Castle display, and a Mickey Mouse marionette show inside a specially-built Mickey Mouse Theater. Of course, O'Neil's toy department housed a complete line of Walt Disney licensed toys as well. Toy ads throughout the *Akron Beacon Journal* during that holiday season featured Mickey Mouse toys in stock at nearly every store downtown—clearly the must-have toys of the 1934 Christmas season. Making the Disney cartoon experience complete, O'Neil's also featured moving figures in their toy display windows along Main Street to correspond with the in-store Mickey Mouse attractions. The next holiday season, in 1935, O'Neil's re-used their Mickey Mouse Castle display on the second floor as well as the Mickey Mouse mechanical figures in their showcase windows.

1935 saw another outstanding Christmas attraction, again from O'Neil's. In addition to the Mickey Mouse Castle display, O'Neil's also offered a "ride" on the Submarine Three-1. Much like the 1933 attraction of a zeppelin "ride," (and perhaps even re-using the metal hull of the zeppelin), children were invited to enjoy "a thrilling adventure in a submarine that is so realistic you can feel the motion of the boat and hear water as it slaps against the side of the ship." Admission was twenty-five cents which also got participants a surprise package. O'Neil's was turning out to be the frontrunner in offering Christmas attractions that captured every child's imagination. The other downtown department stores faced a formidable challenge if they wanted to match the quality of O'Neil's' walk-throughs.

Polsky's in 1935 designated the toyland on the store's fourth floor a Toy Circus, complete with two live clowns! Children were invited to pay BoBo the Clown twenty-five cents and he would pull out a surprise package from a magic box. Next, Bobo gave kids tickets to have his brother JoJo the Clown take their photo, and place it inside a pin to wear! On Polsky's second floor was a citywide yo-yo tournament, free to all participants. And, Polsky's also hosted Akron's Junior League in 1935 whose members performed a stage play for children, the story of *Snow White and the Seven Dwarfs* [sic] for just twenty five cents. Also in 1935, Yeager's, over on South Howard Street, was attempting to lure new shoppers and reward loyal customers with their own elaborate Toyland. Not only did Yeager's advertise Shirley Temple dolls, and offer greetings from Santa Claus, but they also encouraged shoppers to see the characters painted on their walls. A new mural on the wall of Yeager's store featured characters, from Hungarian-American fairy tale writers and illustrators Maud and Miska Petersham, depicting the story of the soldier boy Háry János and his horse Get-A-Way. Entertainment appropriate for children was different in the 1930s, wasn't it? Downtown retailer Kresge's also joined the race to attract shopper's attention by exploiting a modern technology. Their 1935 event included inviting children to come down to the store and speak with Santa Claus. St. Nick and the children's voices would then be broadcast on WJW, a local radio station. Hearing your child's voice on the radio would be the "thrill of a lifetime" the store promised.

Circus attractions and trained animal acts were popular in the 1930s. In 1936, O'Neil's second floor toyland took on a youngster-pleasing, circus theme again; it was a motif they had used in the past. What was new however was the store's inclusion of trained animal acts. Kiddies were invited to see Ginger the Wonder Goat walk a two-inch pole five feet off the ground. It was promised Ginger would also walk a barrel and perform many other tricks. In addition, there was Susie, a trained dog, who would dive from a spiral ladder, Boots—the acrobatic dog, and Salome—a performing pig. As if this wasn't enough, O'Neil's also featured the famous ventriloquist Madame Dolores Shane with her friend Leander. In 1936, Polsky's also embraced a circus theme in their store's toyland. In 1940, O'Neil's repeated the big top theme with life-size mannequins and animals. The display included a clown

Here's Get-a-Way
and Ha'ry Ja'nos

. . . the wooden Hungarian soldier boy with only one arm and
his friend, the old steed "Get-a-Way"—just before they were
made brand new and shiny—from the fairy tale of MAUD and
MISKA PETERSHAM! SEE THEM IN THEIR STORY
DEPICTED ON YEAGER'S TOYLAND MURALS!

. . . and Santa Will Be Here, too!

November 25, 1935 newspaper ad for Get-a-Way & Ha'ry Ja'nos story murals in
Yeager's Toyland.

Polsky's Toyland Is Open Now . . . Second Floor!

See TOM
the Talking
HORSE

*Get a Surprise
Gift Package!*

Yes, indeed, Tom really
TALKS. Come see for
yourself, ask him ques-
tions. And get a won-
derful gift package. All
this fun for just

24c

plus tax

November 17, 1942 newspaper ad for Polsky's
"Tom the Talking Horse" attraction.

band, animated elephants, and the freak show's sword swal-
lower, fat lady, rubberneck man, and laughing man. O'Neil's also
welcomed real life clowns Golly and Nikko to greet children on
the store's second floor. Cleverly, O'Neil's storefront windows
this same year were also filled with a circus themed display.

At Christmas in 1941, adults were undoubtedly distracted
by the news events of the day including the early December
bombing of Pearl Harbor by the Japanese and President
Roosevelt's announcement of the Unites States' entry into global
war. Probably by way of a comforting distraction, Polsky's filled
their second floor toyland with a display featuring the brand-new
Walt Disney animated movie *Dumbo*.

During the World War II years, the most interesting
Christmas attraction belonged to Polsky's. In 1942, the store
introduced Tom the Talking Horse—an attraction that needed
to be seen to be believed. Children were invited to share their

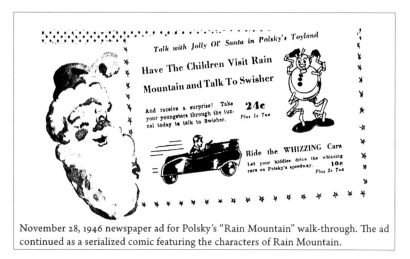

Talk with Jolly Ol' Santa in Polsky's Toyland

Have The Children Visit Rain Mountain and Talk To Swisher

And receive a surprise! Take your youngsters through the tunnel today to talk to Swisher.

24c
Plus 1c Tax

Ride the WHIZZING Cars
Let your kiddies drive the whizzing cars on Polsky's speedway.
10c
Plus 2c Tax

November 28, 1946 newspaper ad for Polsky's "Rain Mountain" walk-through. The ad continued as a serialized comic featuring the characters of Rain Mountain.

Christmas wishes with the talking white steed on their way to meet Santa Claus on the store's second floor. Tom the Talking Horse was just the beginning of a long line of interactive, conversing Christmas attractions in Akron.

Children at Polsky's during the 1940s could ride a miniature merry-go-round in the toyland for a small admission price. Starting in 1944 at O'Neil's, kids were able to take indoor rides for a small admission price on a miniature PT boat, the speedy torpedo vessels used during WWII by the Americans in the conflict in the South Pacific. In 1946 the PT boat attraction was replaced by a mini-replica of the Baltimore & Ohio steamliner train, Shenandoah, which wound its way through a second floor display of a Christmas tree forest.

In 1946, Polsky's filled their toyland attraction space with a fantasy display beyond belief. Calling the display Rain Mountain, the attraction was based on an adventure story that unfolded in a comic strip that ran in the daily newspaper through the holiday season. The outlandish fantasy story encouraged readers to visit Polsky's to see the display that continued the adventures in front of them. Not to be outdone, O'Neil's ran their own serialized comic called *Eskimo Village News* in the daily newspaper during the holidays in 1948. The comic gave information and updates about the Eskimo attraction on O'Neil's second floor. The following year,

November 25, 1949 newspaper ad for O'Neil's "Shenandoah" train attraction.

in 1949, O'Neil's repeated the Eskimo village attraction inside the downtown store however, the comic did not run in the newspaper again.

Still creating popular Christmas attractions, Yeager's department store in 1948 promoted their own toyland circus display. The attraction consisted of three animal acts—*Canine Capers* in which intelligent dogs, Boots and Saddles from Hollywood, performed clever acts; *Monkeyshines* in which a funny monkey named Julia played the piano and rode a bicycle; and *Cockatoo Cut-ups!* in which a trained bird performed tricks.

Contrary to what one might expect, the era of the grandest in-store Christmas attractions doesn't coincide with that became the golden era of downtown window displays—the 1950s and '60s. Perhaps retailers budgets only allowed for major expenditures in one of these areas—but not both—most years. So while the 1930s and '40s seemed to be a high point for in-store toyland Christmas attractions, these efforts waned during the years that the window displays grew grander and more breathtaking. Nevertheless, there were still some in-store attractions of note—several of which were talking attractions.

At Polsky's in 1950, instead of Tom the Talking Horse, children found a new conversing friend in Rudolph the Red-Nosed Reindeer. Santa's favorite reindeer was located on the store's second floor and engaged anyone who visited him in a conversation. Rudolph was popular enough to return to Polsky's each holiday season through 1953.

While Santa Claus was busy arriving in ever-increasingly thrilling modes of transportation all over town, O'Neil's second floor toyland in 1956 hosted a new guest, Krazy Kris the Klown, a giant, wooden, comical clown figure "...whose loose-jointed antics will leave you chuckling," promised the store's ad. In 1958, Polsky's offered a similarly themed experience with a new Christmas attraction—Jingles the Clown, a friend to Santa Claus. Children who visited Jingles could also purchase surprise packages for twenty five or fifty cents, and rides on the store's merry-go-round were a mere ten cents. Meeting Jingles the Clown became an exciting Christmas opportunity and he returned to Polsky's each year through 1962.

At Christmas in 1962, O'Neil's introduced downtown shoppers to a bit of clever marketing that combined a little thrill with convenience. The store promoted a new one-way express elevator to the store's upper floor that embraced the space race. The Rocket Express brought kids to Santaland with space age speed. Akron's Christmas was as modern as they come. And yes—the elevator operators were dressed as astronauts. The Rocket Express elevators were repeated for several additional holiday seasons.

Akron's first indoor mall, Summit Mall in Fairlawn was officially opened in 1965. To launch their first Christmas shopping season, the mall invited children to walk through a magical display of Alice in Wonderland, for a twenty-five cent admission. The following year, in 1967, Summit Mall created an irresistible Christmas attraction with a puppet show, a celebrity autograph signing, and a deer farm with more than thirty live animals to pet and feed in the mall's center. In 1968 at Summit Mall, children were invited to see an Armed Forces Christmas display, and visit the animals in their deer farm again.

Akron's children also had the option in 1967 to witness Santa Claus riding atop a live elephant as he entered Chapel Hill Mall. In 1968 at Chapel Hill, of course children were eager to experience something new—a twenty-foot-tall talking snowman!

THE TREE OF LIGHTS

In 1966, downtown retailers were anxious about Akron's shoppers being lured to suburban shopping centers and malls. The active merchants group, The Downtown Association of Akron, put into motion a brand new Christmas attraction that is still discussed nearly fifty years later. Renting twelve carbon arc lights (think: giant searchlights or spotlights used at celebrity events), the association placed them in a circle and focused the beams to meet at a mutual point, high up in the sky, about three miles up. The Tree of Lights, as it was called, created a brilliant luminous holiday tree glowing above downtown. Inspired with the Christmas spirit, shoppers had the perfect reason to come downtown, check out the overhead display, and hopefully do some shopping.

The Tree of Lights was advertised as taking place on three consecutive evenings, Thursday, Friday, and Saturday, November 24th, 25th, and 26th, 1966. That was Thanksgiving evening and the following two days—the official start of the holiday shopping season. The breathtaking sight was so spectacular, it was photographed for the front page of the *Beacon Journal* on Friday of that week in 1966. If the lights display was repeated today, where in the city would you go to observe the fantastic sight?

November 23, 1966 newspaper ad for The Tree of Lights.

THE STORY OF ARCHIE THE TALKING SNOWMAN

At the close of the decade, Polsky's created one of their most elaborate walk-through displays inside the second floor auditorium. In 1969, children were entertained by the Winter Wonderland walk-through display, a psychedelic fantasy exhibition that included several stuffed dogs in humorous settings. There was a bulldog suffering from indigestion after enjoying his holiday meal, dogs dancing and canines in a band at a discotheque, a gas station setting with a dog making an inspection under a car's hood with a poodle behind the wheel. There was even an outdoor winter scene complete with canines downhill skiing and one unfortunate dog requiring medical attention after a nasty spill. Other dogs can be seen caroling outside a ski chalet. The fantasy animal display was located within a larger display consisting of a pink and silver forest with lively music and dancing trees. As always, visitors could chat with Santa Claus at the end of the journey. Polsky's was so pleased with the crowds that showed up on the Winter Wonderland display's opening day that they commented in the following day's newspaper that they'd hosted more than nine thousand visitors, with a queue that extended outside the store! Polsky's apologized for the long lines and reminded shoppers that the walk-through would be open through Christmas.

The following years, in 1970 and '71, Polsky's advertised their psychedelic Winter Wonderland Christmas attraction once again. "Come see the magic mirror, the day-glo forest, the crystal forest, the animated animals and of course, Santa," read a newspaper ad for the walk-through. The promise of this psychedelic experience seems to capture a very specific moment in our cultural history.

For the rest of the '70s at Polsky's, the window displays were drastically reduced and patrons were promised entertainment inside the store. Upstairs in Polsky's second floor display during the 1970s, children saw fantasy displays of Eskimos, polar bears, and later on delightful forest animals.

Throughout the 1970s, O'Neil's store still welcomed visitors to greet their store Santa Claus. They also began putting the previous year's animated window displays on exhibition in their fifth floor Santa's Walkaround Wonderland. The best of these was the 1978

November 25, 1969 newspaper ad for Polsky's "Winter Wonderland" walk-through.

gnomes window display which reappeared in 1979 inside the store. However these were lean years for O'Neil's. Understandably, they stayed focused on sales rather than entertainment at Christmas.

The last hurrah for O'Neil's Christmas attractions came in 1984. In the newly re-modeled interior of O'Neil's, visitors could see brand new storybook figures in the upstairs walk-through, Santa's Wonderland. "Come board O'Neil's brand new Rocket Ship that will whisk you through our time tunnel into magical lands that are waiting for you at O'Neil's Downtown on the Fourth Floor," read their newspaper ad that year. The new walk-through was described as a series of large displays much like the elaborate animated displays from the golden age of O'Neil's windows in the 1950s and '60s. There was a Mother Goose Land scene including the characters The Old Lady Who Lived in a Shoe, Three Men in a Tub, the Three Little Pigs, and Mother Goose herself. Another scene displayed *Alice in Wonderland* characters including Alice at the Mad Hatter's tea party and the Queen of Hearts. Another display featured Never, Never Land with Peter Pan, Wendy, and Captain Hook figures set in a fourteen-foot pirate ship at Skull Mountain. Children could also see a display sharing the story of *The Wizard of Oz* with the familiar Yellow Brick Road, and everyone's favorite characters Dorothy, Tin Man, Lion, Scarecrow and the Castle of Oz. In another scene, mechanical, moving Cabbage Patch dolls were on display in a farm setting. And, children could also see a display of Care Bears as they crossed a rainbow towards the castle. This huge investment in money and space within O'Neil's was an effort to grab Akron residents' attention to shop downtown—now or never.

The following year, O'Neil's took advantage of the previous holiday season's investment in the unique character Happy News Boy for the windows. In 1985, O'Neil's offered free admission for a musical stage production based on the story of Happy News Boy. Their advertising proclaimed,

> **"Happy the Little news Boy brings the gift of laughter to the home of the richest, meanest man in town! Come see our new 1985 Christmas musical and let Happy capture**

November 26, 1987 newspaper ad for O'Neil's "Santa's Enchanted Forest" attraction. The text mentions performances by renowned puppeteer George Latshaw and the original "Santas by Marina" exhibit.

your heart and put you in the holiday spirit. Meet Happy in person after the show and get a Happy Times News Reporter Hat and a Happy Snowflake as your gift."

The thirty-minute musical was staged in O'Neil's Downtown Showplace on Two, and was performed at various intervals on certain days through the holiday season. This year, O'Neil's also brought back their new displays from 1984 in the walk-around attraction inside the store, including the Cabbage Patch dolls, Care Bears, Peter Pan, Wizard of Oz, Alice in Wonderland, and the Mother Goose fairy tale characters. The next year, in 1986, O'Neil's repeated both the musical stage production with Happy News Boy and the walk-through attraction with the popular children's storybook characters.

In 1987, O'Neil's was eager to show off more re-modeling they had done and improvements made to their Christmas attractions. The store invested $50,000 to help upgrade and refurbish and expand their walk-through, Santa's Enchanted Forest. The new Christmas fantasy land was moved to the third floor, in an area twice as large as the previous fourth floor location. The walk-through included the same animatronic figures and displays purchased in 1984 which consisted of the classic characters from *The Wizard of Oz, Alice in Wonderland, Peter Pan, Mother Goose,* The Old Woman who Lived in a Shoe, the Three Little Pigs, Three Men in a Tub, Care Bears, Cabbage Patch dolls, as well as Santa in his sleigh. There was also an elaborate train display which included three large scale trains in an alpine setting.

To appeal to the adult visitors at O'Neil's, there was also a display of nineteen cloth and ceramic figures of Santa Claus and international gift-givers throughout the world. "Santas By Marina" as these figures were known, were created by the Columbus artist, Marina Cantlon. The exhibit entitled "Santas from the Past, to the Present" allowed store customers to buy their own Cantlon-made limited edition Santas. Each figure was thoroughly researched and came with a scroll detailing the figure's historical accuracy.

In 1987, O'Neil's also hired the firm of Newell-Petrone Inc. of Cleveland to write, stage, and perform a brand new thirty-minute musical, *The Adventures of Albert, the Flying Reindeer* in the new one hundred seat Ice Castle Theater inside the store. Despite the obvious pull of customers into the downtown location, O'Neil's future was in dire jeopardy. As difficult as it may be to admit, people were changing their shopping habits permanently and the appeal of Christmas attractions downtown was no longer sufficient to keep merchants open year round.

The following year, in 1988, O'Neil's repeated this grand labor of love for Akron's children. Once again and for the last time, children and adults were invited to walk through the display of children's storybook animated figures, gaze at the Santas by Marina, enjoy the musical production of *The Adventures of Albert, the Flying Reindeer,* talk with the giant sized Raggedy Ann, and get a photo with Santa Claus. After 1988, Christmases downtown were never quite as bright.

The best, most dazzling Christmas attractions in Akron in the 1970s were to be found at Rolling Acres. The first year the mall opened, in 1975, a new talking figure debuted, the fifteen-foot RA the Friendly Rolling Acres Giant. Patrons also enjoyed conversing with RA the following year, in 1976 as well.

During the next three Christmas seasons at Rolling Acres (1977-79), children were treated to a brand new mall-wide attraction, Disney's Magical Kingdom of Christmas. Not only was Santa Claus there but so were Mickey Mouse, Donald Duck, Pluto, and Snow White and the Seven Dwarfs [sic]. The famous magician Harry Albacker entertained with magical feats during selected times. All of this took place within the mall and in the shadow of Cinderella's Castle and other Disney displays. Disney's Magical Kingdom of Christmas was repeated in 1978, and included a 50th birthday celebration for Mickey Mouse.

During the holiday of 1980 at Rolling Acres, another beautiful production was underway. The mall assembled a floor-to-ceiling, stylized Christmas tree near the north fountains beneath the stunning skylight. The amazing tree held four-foot animatronic figures and views within four tiers of display space. The scenes within the tree included animated elves, yuletide characters, and

ROLLING ACRES MALL

HEY KIDS!

COME ON OUT & SEE
SANTA UNVEIL RĀ OUR
15 FOOT FRIENDLY TALKING GIANT.
TOMORROW 9:30 A.M.

- ★ SEE & HEAR RĀ WELCOME SANTA TO SANTA VILLAGE . . .
- ★ MEET SANTA & TALK WITH RĀ.
- ★ FREE CANDY CANES FOR THE KIDS
- ★ FREE RĀ MASKS
- ★ PHOTOS AVAILABLE WITH SANTA
- ★ JOIN SANTA, RĀ, SANTA BELLES, DIXIE LAND BAND, IN A CHRISTMAS PARADE AT 9:30 A.M.

FUN, MUSIC & EXCITEMENT.

CHRISTMAS STARTS HERE WITH 78 GREAT STORES AND SERVICES. CHECK THE FOLLOWING PAGES FOR ALL YOUR NEEDS. ONE STOP SHOPPING.

SANTA'S & RĀ'S HOURS

NOV. 26 . . . . 9:30 A.M.-9 P.M.
NOV. 27 . . . . 10:00 A.M.-9 P.M.
MON. THRU FRIDAYS 11:00 A.M.-9 P.M.
SATURDAYS . . . . 10:00 A.M.-9 P.M.
SUNDAYS . . . . 12 NOON-6 P.M.
DEC. 24 . . . . 11:00 A.M.-5:30 P.M.

RIDE THE SANTA EXPRESS

BEHIND SANTA VILLAGE

ROLLING ACRES MALL

ROLLING ACRES MALL On Romig Road . . . in southwest Akron, near Barberton
A joint venture of Forest City Rental Properties Corporation and Richard B. Buchholzt

November 25, 1976 newspaper ad for Rolling Acres Mall's talking giant, RA.

Mrs. Claus, among other sights. Also within the tree, one could see lights, colorful ornaments, and a shiny star at the top. Promoted by the theme "Christmas is For You," Rolling Acres' unique display was designed by the Walter Swartz Design Group of New Jersey. Two local artists Robin White and Dennis McCabe implemented the design project at the mall. According to promotional materials, it took two months to assemble the giant tree inside Rolling Acres. Local display artist White was in charge of its construction while artist McCabe handled the final detail work on the tree. The Santa Express kiddie train ride was also on hand at Rolling Acres in the early 1980s. The trips began at the fountain in the North Concourse and looped around the new giant tree display. The elaborate tree display was re-installed each holiday season through 1984.

By the mid-1980s, much of the competitive spirit between retailers was in the past. Rolling Acres celebrated the holidays with the theme "Jingle Bell Christmas" from 1985-88 offering children free jingle bells to help ring in Santa's annual arrival at the mall. In 1986, the mall's events included Akron's Children's Theater performances of *The Bell*. During the 1990s, Christmas at Rolling Acres embraced themes of the Magic of Christmas, Santa's Starlight Arrival, and a gingerbread-inspired fantasy land. For several years, the mall hosted musical performances by the Akron Youth Symphony and dancers from the Cleveland Ballet. Despite the elegance and high cultural events, stories and rumors about violence and crime wrecked the mall's reputation, making it nearly impossible to bring in shoppers from all over the city anymore. The last year the mall advertised about its Santa Claus was 2003. Rolling Acres officially closed in 2008.

In the 1970s at Summit Mall, the main attractions at Christmas were beautifully staged puppet shows. However the most memorable attraction occurred on the day after Thanksgiving in 1978. Mall ads encouraged children to claim free space balloons and get their photo taken with unnamed special guests. Although the ad didn't name the special guests, perhaps creating a certain air of mystery and excitement, the photo incorporated in the ad was unmistakably that of Darth Vader, C3-PO, and R2-D2—everyone's favorite robots and villain from the hot movie, *Star Wars!* Though *Star Wars* photo opportunities are more common these days, in 1978 this rare event would have been a lure like none other.

In 1982, Summit Mall embraced patriotic themes for its Christmas decorations including "A Williamsburg Colonial Christmas," in celebration of our nation's traditional colonial past. The mall's Santa sat in a replica of a late 1700s-era sleigh. For the youngsters, Summit Mall installed a large gingerbread-style house guarded by a costumed character named Chris Mouse. On the Friday after Thanksgiving, Chris Mouse was joined by more costumed characters including Strawberry Shortcake, Sea World characters, the Kay Bee Toys Toy Soldier, and of course, Santa himself. In 1983 and '84, the traditional Colonial Christmas was repeated.

1984 also saw much excitement at Summit Mall. Children were encouraged to experience the fun of Hanna Barbera animation by visiting with costumed characters from their favorite Saturday morning cartoon shows. A live production entitled *Scooby's Magical Christmas* was staged and included the costumed characters of Scooby Doo, Yogi Bear, Jabber Jaw, and more. "Ring in the Yuletide with Hanna-Barbera Magic. Scooby's up to his old tricks again as Yogi Bear and Jabber Jaws [sic] try to show old Scooby-Doo the true meaning of the holiday season," read an ad promoting the show.

In the following year, Summit Mall returned to the kiddie favorite of cartoon characters with their latest Christmas attraction. Another stage production was launched entitled *A Smurfy Christmas*. The free performance included costumed characters from the popular line of toys and the cartoon show including Papa Smurf, Clumsy Smurf, Brainy Smurf, and Baby Smurf. "Papa and Clumsy try to convince Brainy that there really are a lot of nice things about Christmas," stated an ad that encapsulated the holiday production.

For several years in the 1990s, Summit Mall also hosted The Holiday Tree Festival, Akron's much-loved fundraiser for Akron Children's Hospital. The height of Summit Mall's Christmas attractions may be in the past although the mall continues to offer photos with Santa Claus each year. As of this writing, Summit Mall continues as a thriving retail center in Fairlawn.

Of course, Chapel Hill Mall was the home to Archie the Talking Snowman in the 1970s, '80s, and '90s. By the Christmas season of 2003, Chapel Hill had hosted Archie the Talking Snowman for the thirty-sixth year in a row. However, promotions for the Frosty One were at an all time low with barely a mention throughout the entire months of November and December in the local newspaper. Archie's popularity had seen better days—and so had Chapel Hill Mall.

By 2004, the world of retail had changed immeasurably since the mall's opening in the mid-1960s. Consumer habits had changed and brick-and-mortar stores had to adapt to retain customers. Lasting longer than any other one attraction in Akron, Archie the Snowman was retired after 2003 when the Tennessee-based corporation CBL & Associates purchased Chapel Hill Mall from its original owners, Richard Buchholzer and Forest City Enterprises. But Archie's retirement was not permanent.

YULETIDE YAKKERS: TALKING ATTRACTIONS BEFORE & AFTER ARCHIE

Did you assume Archie the Snowman was Akron's only talking Christmas attraction? The fact is, the twenty-foot-tall snowman is just one of at least seven talking characters featured in retail spaces in Akron during the holidays over the past seventy years. Fasten your seat belts for a stunning ride through the history of interactive—and potentially scary—inanimate objects.

Polsky's, downtown on Main Street, was the first to feature a talking Christmas attraction. Starting in 1942, children were invited to the store's second floor toy department to meet Tom the Talking Horse, a white steed tended by a pretty riding mistress. Polsky's placed enigmatic advertisements for the new holiday attraction, "Come see for yourself," the ads curiously proclaimed, purposefully never making it clear if the horse was a live animal, a mechanical device, or a large stuffed toy. Luring children and their parents into downtown department stores to participate in a fantasy experience was a firmly established tradition since the 1920s in Akron. This next generation of Akron's children required a higher standard to appeal to their curiosity. And Polsky's attempted to meet the challenge.

Tom the Talking Horse proved to be a popular, must-see yuletide experience and he remained a featured Christmas attraction at Polsky's from 1942-49. Although descriptions of the horse are scarce, it is believed Tom's voice came courtesy of a man hidden within the surrounding display. For an additional twenty-five cents,

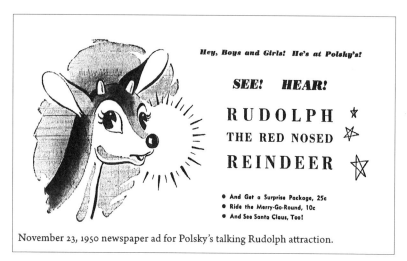

November 23, 1950 newspaper ad for Polsky's talking Rudolph attraction.

children received a toy surprise after their conversation with Tom.

In 1950, Polsky's replaced Tom the Talking Horse with another talking attraction, Rudolph the Red-Nosed Reindeer in the store's second floor auditorium. "See him, talk to him…he'll answer your questions and give you a gift package too!" all for twenty-five cents. Conversing with Santa's most popular reindeer at Polsky's was a crowd-pleasing and unique Christmas attraction for four years in Akron (1950-53.) Of course, Rudolph was a familiar holiday character to youngsters by 1950. The reindeer with the crimson nose was created in 1939 as a character for a promotional booklet by Montgomery Ward stores. Later, the character was the star of a 1944 Technicolor cartoon that played at movie theaters. Then Rudolph was the subject of a hit song recorded in 1949 by the singing cowboy Gene Autry. (However, the animated TV special about Rudolph, produced by Rankin/Bass wasn't created until 1964.) How exciting it must have been to chat with everyone's favorite holiday underdog.

After four years with Rudolph, Polsky's returned to the previously successful chatty Christmas attraction, Tom the Talking Horse. The 1940s popular verbose white steed was available at Polsky's to make memories with another generation of the youngest in Akron. Starting in 1954, Tom the Talking Horse joined Santa Claus to greet visitors on the store's second floor toyland.

ONEILS

How the Magic Pine Cone Became a Talking Christmas Tree

Just outside Santa's shop in the enchanted forest, at the top of a tall pine tree, there grew a little pine cone . . . a magic pine cone. One day it fell, Kerplunk, right into Santa's long white beard. So Santa brought it to O'Neil's, where with tender care it grew and grew and grew . . . into a wonderful talking tree. Ever hear a Christmas Tree talk? You will if you visit O'Neil's Fifth Floor.

November 30, 1966 newspaper ad for O'Neil's talking Christmas Tree attraction.

Tom would attract visitors for the rest of the decade.

Rising to meet the competition across Main Street and across town, O'Neil's created their first talking Christmas attraction in 1965. On the fifth floor of O'Neil's downtown store, children were invited to converse with a talking Christmas tree. By 1965, O'Neil's strategy to attract attention for potential shoppers was fierce— not only were Akron's skies filled with helicopters delivering Santa Clauses, but celebrity appearances and Christmas attractions wooed holiday shoppers to every retail location in greater-Akron. Also in 1965, the brand new Summit Mall was opening its doors for the first time and in 1966 Chapel Hill Mall opened. Shopping centers and plazas had already chipped away at the foundation of Polsky's and O'Neil's shoppers' loyalty. The future of downtown's retailers was looking dark.

Part of O'Neil's solution to entice shoppers downtown at the holidays was the talking Christmas tree. In 1966, O'Neil's placed an ad in the local newspaper that created a backstory for their talking tree, explaining How the Magic Pine Cone Became a Talking Christmas Tree:

> "Just outside Santa's shop in the enchanted forest at the top of a tall pine tree, there grew a little pine cone...a magic pine cone. One day it fell, Kerplunk, right into Santa's long white beard. So Santa brought it to O'Neil's, where with tender care it grew and grew and grew...into a wonderful talking tree. Ever hear a Christmas tree talk? You will if you visit O'Neil's Fifth Floor."

Another ad fills out the description of what O'Neil's Christmas attraction looked like in 1969, "Follow the Magic Path, through the Enchanted Forest, over the Wishing Stream 'til you come to the Talking Christmas Tree. Stay awhile for a friendly Christmas word or two...and then on to Santa's special place in Wonderland." O'Neil's talking Christmas tree began standing tall in 1965 and continued each Christmas season for eight years (1965-72.)

It was into this historical and hallucinatory context that Archie the Talking Snowman first entered the fracas. Archie was created to attract attention and draw people to Chapel Hill Mall starting in 1968. Was a two-story, speaking snowman interesting enough to out talk a chatty Christmas tree, a rambling reindeer, and a hoarse horse? Honestly, history speaks for itself—Archie occupied Chapel Hill for thirty-six years and still dominates the conversation about talking Christmas attractions. But Archie wasn't the last attempt in Akron at talking Christmas attractions.

Akron's suburban children didn't have to go all the way downtown to speak with a magical Christmas tree—starting in 1968, youngsters went to Summit Mall in Fairlawn to see an enchanted, erudite Christmas tree in the mall's center court! That's right, for a half dozen years in Akron in the late '60s through the early '70s, our children had the opportunity to engage Christmas trees in conversation in two different retail locations! Still not enough? During the 1970s, the Stow Jaycees put together an annual Christmas display and attraction on Fishcreek Road as a fundraiser for their organization which also included a talking Christmas tree!

Starting in 1972, O'Neil's operated another talking attraction by adding a talking Raggedy Ann doll to the Santa Land walkthrough experience in their downtown store. By the holiday season in 1973, the nine-foot-tall rag doll seated in a chair replaced the talking Christmas tree. Just like the other speaking attractions, the larger-than-life doll asked children about their holiday wishes and engaged everyone in conversation who had the courage to stop and greet her.

Archie the Snowman may have frightened his share of Akron's youngsters, but O'Neil's Raggedy Ann traumatized quite a few herself. Akron resident Scott Robishaw confessed to me that his memories of visiting the talking rag doll were less than pleasant. Speaking of Raggedy Ann, he said,

> "Less enchanting [than Archie]; she was horrifying. There [Raggedy Ann] sat on that little porch in that red gingham dress, that lace apron, and Mary Jane shoes with a mangy little white dog on her lap. A mop of bright red hair on her large flat head (five feet across!) that would pivot slowly and she would stare at you with big black unblinking eyes. You had to pass by her to enter into Santa's Village and eventually see Santa. With her weird smiling triangle mouth she would ask intrusive questions like 'How are you today?' and 'Do you know what you're going to ask from Santa?' It's still disturbing years later."

Despite frightening some children, Raggedy Ann remained a featured attraction each holiday season at O'Neil's until the store closed (1972-88.) The seventeen-year legacy of the Raggedy Ann doll stands as the second longest-lasting talking Christmas attraction in Akron's history, behind Archie the Snowman.

An interesting footnote in the legacy of O'Neil's Raggedy Ann

O'Neil's talking Raggedy Ann doll on display at the Marble Museum, Akron Ohio, 2014. Photo: Dominic Caruso.

THE STORY OF ARCHIE THE TALKING SNOWMAN

doll includes a Hollywood connection. Former O'Neil's display department employee Lawrence Nixon recalled that when the movie *A Christmas Story* was shooting in nearby Cleveland in 1983, O'Neil's display department received a phone call from the film company's props department looking for Christmas decorations to provide visual details while filming the background scenes. Nixon said they loaned the film crew quite a bit of their stuff—including the giant Raggedy Ann doll. The cult holiday film *A Christmas Story* has only grown in popularity in the three decades since its initial release, boosted tremendously by the tradition of the movie's airing during a 24-hour marathon each Christmas Eve since 1997 on cable TV's TNT (or TBS) network.

Keen viewers of the movie may have spotted a larger-than-life size Raggedy Ann doll sitting silently in one background scene for just a brief moment of screen time. In the shot following the scene where Ralphie stands in line, talks with Santa Claus, crawls back up the slide to ask for his Red Rider BB gun, and slides down the chute into the pool of foam, Ralphie is seen exiting the attraction with his family on the store's ground floor. While the family walks away from the display area, in the background can be seen the Raggedy Ann doll. It should be noted that another store, Hixons Inc. of Lakewood lays claim to owning the oversized Raggedy Ann doll that appears in *A Christmas Story*. However, photos of both O'Neil's doll and Hixons' doll show differences in appearance from the one that appeared in the 1983 movie. Who's story would you rather believe?

If young Akronites were brave enough to approach Archie and Raggedy Ann, there was another standard for courage set in 1975. The newly opened Rolling Acres mall introduced a new Christmas attraction in 1975, RA the Friendly Rolling Acres Giant. Pronounced "Ray," the fifteen-foot-tall talking male figure was a physical representation of the mall's personified logo. If you are thinking RA the Friendly Rolling Acres Giant sounds like an Archie rip-off, you're half right. The new Rolling Acres mall was developed by Richard B. Buchholzer with his partners Forest City Enterprises, the same development team that opened Chapel Hill

Mall. Since they also ran Chapel Hill Mall, RA the Friendly Giant is less a rip-off and more of an attempt to capture lighting in a bottle twice. Undoubtedly, Rolling Acres was looking to capitalize on a similar larger-than-life, awe-inspiring mascot during the holiday season. A 1975 Rolling Acres newspaper advertisement claimed, "Santa will give all the children a gift: a RA the Friendly Giant of Rolling Acres face mask." At the time of this writing, no amount of Googling unearthed an image of what these masks looked like! RA, the Friendly Talking Giant stood for a second year in the center of the new mall during the holiday season of 1976, however it is unclear if the behemoth existed much longer than that.

CHRISTMAS COMICS

One of the more clever promotional tools used by Akron's downtown department stores at Christmas was the serialized ad and comic. During three different holiday seasons, O'Neil's and Polsky's made the extra effort to hire writers and artists to create exciting serial stories to run in the local newspaper. The comics functioned as more than mere advertising and were a narrative device connecting their in-store Christmas displays with a fantasy holiday experience. Children and adults could follow along with the story each day in the newspaper, and they were encouraged to come downtown and visit the store to experience the walk-through display related to the story again and again for themselves. What an exiting time to live (and read the newspaper) in Akron.

The first example of a store promoting their Christmas attractions by means of a serial story occurred in 1928. It was the first holiday season for the M. O'Neil Company in their new location on the corner of Main and State Street. The newly built store offered expanded floor space for each department as well as a large auditorium on the second floor. In their new auditorium, O'Neil's established their first in-store walk-through display for the holiday season. In 1928, the breathtaking display was entitled The Enchanted Forest, a fantasy exhibit with elves, fairies, animals of the forest, and more, and it was a walk-through wonderland for visitors to experience on their way to greet Santa Claus.

To promote the first walk-through experience, the store ran

Jack and Betty
In The Enchanted Forest

"Hey! Hey!" said Somebody—and the Funny Green Man rolled himself up in a ball and rolled right out of sight! "What a relief," said Jack, and Betty gave him an excited poke as she spied the fattest, roundest little brownie imaginable—all dressed in bright red, with hundreds of little gold bells that sang a merry tune as the little red Brownie w a d d l e d about. "Don't mind old Greenie," said Brownie. "You see, he wanted to be Jester, and when he couldn't—he just turned green with envy—but come on, let's go—hurry! hurry!" "Hurry where," said Jack and Betty running as fast as they could to keep up with Red Brownie who was turning cartwheels right up to the Palace Door and down the Big Fairy Hall. "Why, to the Feast of Tarts," said Red Brownie without ever stopping his cartwheels—"ever since the Queen of Hearts started making tarts all Fairy Land has a feast every Christmas time—Hurry Up! We'll be late!"

Tomorrow you'll hear all about the Feast of Tarts that Jack and Betty enjoyed in the Fairy Palace.

November 21, 1928 O'Neil's "Enchanted Forest" serialized adventure.

a text-based serialized adventure story in the daily *Akron Beacon Journal* and the *Akron Times-Press* over several weeks. The adventures featured Betty and Jack's journey through The Enchanted Forest. The children met and interacted with all sorts of fantasy creatures including elves, brownies, a Fairy Queen, the rabbit Uncle Wiggly, and other talking animals. This clever form of advertising not only sparked the imagination of young folks but appealed to the child inside adults as well. This wasn't the last serialized adventure O'Neil's used to encourage shoppers to visit their store at Christmas time. More on that soon.

After the end of the belt-tightening of The Depression and the uncertainties brought on by World War II, Polsky's decided to try serial comic advertising for their own whimsical Christmas walk-through. In 1946, on Polsky's second floor toyland, for twenty-five cents admission price, children could visit the Rain Mountain fantasy exhibit featuring the surreal character Swisher. Swisher, Betty and Bob were characters first introduced in a serialized comic strip that ran in the daily *Akron Beacon Journal* in November and December 1946 entitled *The Christmas Adventures of Cloudchaser, Betty and Bob*. Much like the serialized text-based story first used by O'Neil's in 1928 to promote their Enchanted Forest display, The Rain Mountain comic sparked readers imaginations about the fantasy adventures of Betty and Bob. Polsky's 1946 promotional comic strip followed the imaginative journey of young Betty and Bob as they took a trip to a cloud city and interact with elves that not only control the weather but assist Santa at the North Pole. This story's fantastical and surreal characters included Cloudchaser, a brave elf; Lillywam, a cloud lamb and companion; Swisher, a cross and gruff creature from Hamp Country; and, the horrible Terrigog with records on the bottoms of his feet! The children's adventure takes them to the exotic locations of Rain Mountain and Thunder Cave in the clouds, as well as Santa's castle at the North Pole and Polsky's department store! The daily comic ran through twenty-two installments and encouraged young visitors to return to the Polsky's in-store display again and again to experience the characters and the fantasy locations they were following in the newspaper each day.

Two years later, O'Neil's returned to serial advertising, this time in paneled comic form to promote their in-store Christmas attraction. In 1948 at O'Neil's, the kiddie B&O steamliner train was moved to the store's fifth floor to accommodate an authentic sprawling Eskimo Village display on the store's second floor toyland area. For thirty-eight cents admission, children could visit this exotic and authentic arctic attraction. The Eskimo village display included Tukto—a real life Eskimo boy, a kayak, an arctic white fox, and rides on an Eskimo sled pulled by a team of dogs.

November 19, 1948 O'Neil's "Eskimo Village News" serialized comic.

The O'Neil's holiday attraction also featured the Husky dog Kamogen and her seven puppies born right there in the store! And here's the kicker: children could visit the real, live Husky dog and her seven puppies in the store! Kamogen's puppies were named Ilena, Sonya, Guto, Kinga, Agoona, Pixik, and Kabloona. Of course, O'Neil's also encouraged children to visit the dogs repeatedly during the holiday season to watch the puppies grow and mature enough to open their eyes, and begin to move about and play. Can you imagine how over-stimulated those dogs must have been as the center of attention in the O'Neil's toyland for weeks on end for thousands of children's entertainment?

The authentic arctic exhibit was not only advertised, but serial single-paneled comics ran in the daily newspaper for weeks promoting the display. The comics entitled *Eskimo Village News* gave details about the Husky dog Kamogen and each of her seven puppies, and Eskimo life including kayaking, dog sleds, and the like. The following year, in 1949, the Eskimo Village attraction at O'Neil's was put on display again on the store's second floor however, the comics were not run again.

SPLENDOR ON A STRING: THE PUPPET SHOWS

Some of the earliest Christmas attractions at the downtown department stores in Akron included puppet shows. Especially in the early days of radio—before television and video games—children's entertainment was much more rare and precious. Puppets could not only hold a child's attention but the colorful characters could tell a story, limited only by one's imagination. The most popular puppet shows were fantasy stories, fairy tales, Christmas adventures, and animal stories. And successful puppet troupes returned year after year to amuse Akron's youngest at holiday time.

The first puppet show advertised to entertain at Christmas in Akron was a Punch and Judy show in 1923, at O'Neil's in their toyland. The puppet characters of Punch and Judy actually have a very long history throughout Western Europe starting in Renaissance Italy and eventually reaching the height of popularity in Victorian England. When in 1923, O'Neil's offered its customers a puppet show in addition to its eye-catching displays of toys and the chance to visit with Santa Claus, it was an aggressive lure to bring shoppers into their store over their competitors. O'Neil's attempts with puppet shows to attract children and thus adult shoppers would not go unnoticed.

When Polsky's decided to enter the annual competition over holiday shoppers by adding Christmas attractions, they too brought in a puppet show. In 1933—the store's second year of offering a Christmas attraction—Polsky's invited the Kingsland Marionettes

Polsky's Wonderful Windows are Open

As has been Polsky's custom for many years, and as important as the holidays themselves, is the opening of Polsky's Christmas windows on Wednesday, Thanksgiving Eve. We're proud to present, for young and old...

By Popular Request ... Right from New York

the Kingsland Marionettes

Complete shows running daily and Sunday, between 11 a. m. and 9 p. m., with the ever-changing fantasies of make-believe, of interest to both adults and children alike.

Bring the Children ... Come Yourself to see the Marionette Show THANKSGIVING DAY ... Laugh with Santa Claus in a NEW Feature ... and Enjoy the Battery of Fantasy Windows that will Recall Christmases Past ...

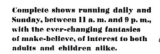

Polsky's

Plan to shop Friday in Akron's largest and finest Toyland on Polsky's Third Floor. Enter directly from High Street.

November 27, 1946 newspaper ad for the Kingsland Marionettes appearance at Polsky's.

November 26, 1947 newspaper ad for O'Neil's String Guild Marionettes performances in the display windows.

to entertain their young patrons. In the store's second floor auditorium, the Kingsland Marionettes performed a show with the puppet, Beppo the Clown, and a story about Santa Claus' around the world adventures. The Kingsland Marionettes were a troupe started by the husband-and-wife team of Mable (Kingsland) and Cedric Head from Boonton, New Jersey, who traveled the country with their popular performances.

Other stores downtown soon followed O'Neil's and Polsky's example by creating their own special events with puppet shows at Christmas time. For example, in 1935, the Akron Dry Goods store brought in Gene Souer's Marionette Show to perform on the store's third floor. There were three different shows performed that Christmas including *The Bag of Gold, Variety Show,* and one about the culturally insensitive literary character "Little Sambo." And, in the late 1930s, O'Neil's attempted to recreate their earlier success with a puppet show Christmas attraction. In the sixth floor music department, O'Neil's hosted performances by Frank Still's Marionettes. In 1938, the troupe performed a story about Robin

Hood, and in 1939, they performed a show based on the classic tale of Aladdin.

The post-war era in Akron brought an expansion to Christmas attractions downtown for the department stores. For five years in a row, Polsky's hosted the renowned Kingsland Marionettes who not only performed but were featured in their windows. By the 1940s, the Kingsland Marionettes, started in the late 1920s, were a puppet troupe of great reputation and popularity. Polsky's ads of the era herald how lucky Akron was to welcome back the troupe each Christmas after headlining shows in cross country tours during the rest of the year. To highlight the featured Kingsland Marionettes, Polsky's showed them off inside their Main Street windows for all to enjoy. At Christmas 1945, the Kingsland Marionettes act included performances of the archery scene from *Robin Hood,* scenes from *Alice in Wonderland,* scenes from *Humpty Dumpty,* six dance routines with Barnacle Bill the sailor, animals and clowns from the circus, and the *Fable of the Desert Wonder.* In a 1946 ad, the Kingsland Marionette's exhausting window performance schedule was made clear, with "complete shows running daily between 11 a.m. and 9 p.m." Their third year in a row at Polsky's, in 1947, the Kingsland Marionettes puppet show in the Main Street windows included a big top theme, complete with a three-ring circus, clowns, animals, and acrobats. In 1948, the Kingsland Marionettes returned with an all-new performance entitled *The Nativity,* a traditional story to amuse the young and old alike. The puppet show, which started over every half hour, told the story of the events in Bethlehem with the three wise men, Mary, Joseph, and the baby Jesus. The Kingsland Marionettes' final year inside Polsky's windows was 1949. That year's puppet show repeated the circus theme, with a new performance every half hour, which included clowns, trapeze artists, elephants, lions, and bareback riders.

Not to be outdone, O'Neil's began their own five-year run of puppet shows in their Main Street windows. Starting in 1946, O'Neil's hosted the Suzari puppeteers with a marionette show entitled *Currier and Ives Ice Ballet.* The 1946 newspaper advertisement for

The magic beauty of Christmas unfolds . . . as always . . . with the opening of O'Neil's Yuletide Windows on Thanksgiving Day. Utterly new and enthralling is our Currier and Ives Ballet, a complete marionette show presented in our Main and State Street window by Suzari puppeteers. Santa and his reindeer are back again . . . of course . . . supported by more Christmas glee in all Main Street windows. Bring the family to see them, right after dinner on Thanksgiving Day!

THE TRADITIONAL THANKSGIVING PARADE IN AKRON IS TO THE WINDOWS AT O'Neil's

O'Neil's is cooperating fully with the government's coal conservation policy.....therefore our windows will be unlighted.....but nonetheless lovely!

November 27, 1946 newspaper ad for the Suzari Marionette's appearance at O'Neil's.

this show reminded readers that O'Neil's is "…in full cooperation of the government's coal conservation policy. The windows are unlighted but nonetheless lovely!" In 1947, after the store rebuilt several of their large windows, O'Neil's filled their Main and Center Street windows with the String Guild Marionettes, with shows at fifteen minute intervals, the most memorable performance being

Santa's Surprise. The following year, in 1948, O'Neil's brought the String Guild Marionettes to their windows once again. That year's puppet show was entitled *Winter Wonderland* a story which sees "...mechanical doll houses unfolding the magic of A Night Before Christmas, the excitement of Christmas morn, clowns performing lively and amusing antics, Santa Claus and his reindeer," and more. In 1949, O'Neil's once again employed The String Guild Marionettes, produced by Wayne Reed, the same popular puppet attraction for O'Neil's windows for a third year in a row. That year's puppet show at O'Neil's was entitled *Puppets on Parade*, at fifteen minute intervals for the downtown crowd's amusement. A newspaper ad of the attraction claimed, "Puppets on Parade is a delightful presentation of light-hearted merriment... amusing, cavorting, characters in a variety of scenes." And, at Christmas 1950 at O'Neil's, the String Guild Marionettes once again returned for all-new shows with their puppets.

Puppet shows would not be popular again during Christmas in downtown Akron department stores until the 1980s. When O'Neil's acquired additional financial investments and used some of the money to boost their Christmas attractions, they allocated some of the money into hiring the world-renowned puppeteer, George Latshaw, to entertain. In 1986, O'Neil's also welcomed George Latshaw's Victorian Puppet Theater to the fourth floor. In 1987, George Latshaw's Ice Castle Puppets performed in Santa's Enchanted Forest display. And, once again in 1988 O'Neil's hosted George Latshaw's puppet show. Puppet aficionados know the name of George Latshaw by reputation. The Northeast Ohio puppeteer literally wrote the book on puppeteering, penning *The Complete Book of Puppetry*. Praised as someone who turned puppetry into an art form, Latshaw "...was widely regarded as a dean of American puppetry" according to his 2006 *New York Times* obituary. Perhaps spreading his reputation even wider, Latshaw's outstanding puppetry was featured in the 1953 movie *Lili*, starring French actress, Leslie Caron.

Although the height of puppet shows as entertainment had already peaked in Akron during the 1940s, when the malls in the area opened—starting in the 1960s—they too were looking to create special events at Christmas time to encourage people to bring their children and shop at the mall. By hiring puppet troupes and building inexpensive but appealing wooden puppet theaters, the new shopping malls could invite shoppers to enjoy the special children's entertainment in the comfort of a indoor facility. This was a clear advantage over the growing popularity of the shopping plazas and strip malls popping up all over town which offered few protections from the holiday season's unpredictable and most likely frigid winter weather conditions. Between the late 1960s and the mid '80s, several local puppeteering groups entertained at local malls during the Christmas season.

The Scollon's Marionettes were a popular attraction at Christmas time, creating new performances each year to entertain local children. The Scollon's Marionettes were a touring puppet group, started by Allie Scollon and her husband Bill, who specialized in shopping mall shows, performing throughout the United States and Canada. In 1967, the Scollon's Marionettes performed two complete stories *The Night Before Christmas* and *The Elves and the Shoemaker* at Summit Mall. In 1968, they performed the show *Alice in Christmasland,* also at Summit Mall. When the brand new Belden Village Mall, opened in 1970 in Canton, they too hired the Scollon's Marionettes at Christmas to perform six shows daily through the holidays. They performed the shows *The Day the North Pole Melted* and *The Nutcracker* which surely lured quite a few parents with their children. In an effort to keep local shoppers from heading south to the new Belden Village Mall, Akron's own Summit Mall also hired the Scollon's Marionettes to entertain with these same two shows, six performances daily, during the month of December 1970.

The Scollon's Marionettes returned to perform at Belden Village Mall during the Christmas season in 1972 and in 1973. It was during the latter year that the performance was entitled *Christmas in Candyland.* Later in 1979, the Scollon's Marionettes performed at Rolling Acres Mall with the show *The Twelve Days of Christmas.*

December 3, 1970 newspaper ad for the Scollon's Marionettes performance of *The Day the North Pole Melted* at Summit Mall.

And, in 1980, Scollon's returned to Rolling Acres with the show *The Christmas Carol.*

The Heiken Puppets, a midwestern traveling troupe also performed holiday shows at the malls. In 1971 at Belden Village Mall, the Heiken Puppets entertained with daily shows, entitled *Peter and the Wolf, Elves and the Shoemaker, The Reluctant Dragon,* and *The Nutcracker.* In 1986, the Heiken Puppets returned to the area, this time to perform at Rolling Acres Mall, with the show *The Nutcracker Suite.*

Creegan Productions is another puppeteering group that performed at Akron's Summit Mall. They entertained at Summit Mall in 1972 with the show *Cinderella at Christmas Time* and again in 1973 with the puppet show *Hansel & Gretel's Magical Winter Forest.* Creegan Productions was a puppet outfit from Steubenville, Ohio, and they not only created their own puppets and theaters but were one of the few companies in the 1970s and 1980s to build mechanical and animatronic figures for department store window displays.

Talented puppeteer Fred Cowan also entertained at Christmas in the area. In 1976, '77, and '78, Cowan's marionettes entertained children and adults alike at Belden Village Mall. Cowan was a renowned puppet builder as well as a performer, having entertained at the White House for Presidents Ford and Carter.

The Eric Norman National Puppet Show came to perform at Belden Village Mall during Christmas time in 1981. Eric and his wife Barbara, from New Jersey, headed the troupe of puppeteers that performed *The Story of the Nutcracker.* The special show featured twenty puppets in a story that lasted three acts. The Norman family of puppeteers still perform, under the name of The National Puppet Theater, headed by Eric's son Steve.

And the Sunshine Marionettes brought an outstanding musical show to Belden Village Mall at the holidays in 1982. The performance featured marionettes specially crafted to resemble famous stars in a Las Vegas-style showcase. The character puppets, handmade by brothers Jim and Gene Andrette from Orlando, included Donny & Marie, Elvis Presley, Phyllis Diller, Dolly Parton, and Tony Orlando and Dawn.

THE STORY OF ARCHIE THE TALKING SNOWMAN

FREE CHILDCARE, WHILE YOU SHOP!

Although many parents today cringe at the thought of dropping off their young ones with strangers in order to go shopping, it was a popular and effective motivation in decades past to lure potential shoppers to stores during gift-giving season. It was common practice for parents to leave their children while they stood in line at the store's walk-through Santa Land experience as well as any queue to sit on Santa's lap. Many parents may have wanted to purchase children's gifts without spoiling the surprise, so, different variations of babysitting provided by retailers served a practical purpose. The following examples are some of the more unique methods stores employed in providing babysitting for shopping parents.

In 1914, O'Neil's advertised an indoor playground on their fifth floor. This attraction included a "competent attendant" urging parents to leave their children in the playground while they shopped elsewhere in the store. The noteworthy attraction was clearly attempting to appeal to parents to make their Christmas shopping experience more carefree, efficient, and easy.

In 1933, Yeager's, one of the leading department stores in downtown, advertised The Storytelling Lady, who held audience with children in the store's auditorium. Parents were encouraged to drop off their children with the Storytelling Lady where they would be entertained, hearing fascinating stories. In exchange, the

November 20, 1961 newspaper ad for Montgomery Ward's "Babysitter" offer.

parents could shop—presumably within Yeager's—with greater convenience and less distraction.

Sensing an opportunity, in 1934 Polsky's ran free admission to holiday short films for children two times daily. The "Santa Claus movies" were promised as sound films—which seems like a bargain considering sound film had only come into commercial availability less than ten years earlier.

By the 1960s and '70s, children's Christmas movie matinees were commonplace throughout greater-Akron. Local plazas, shopping centers, and the new malls, many of which incorporated multi-screen theaters in their complexes, used the proximity of theaters to their advantage. For example, in December 1961,

Montgomery Ward at State Road Shopping Center in Cuyahoga Falls included the distribution of free tickets to kiddie movies at the nearby State Theatre. "Let Montgomery Ward Be Your Babysitter," read their ad's eye-catching advertisement. Though a promise of this sort would certainly raise eyebrows these days, you may be surprised to learn that this promotion was very popular—and was repeated in subsequent years. Whether the youngsters were dropped off or accompanied by an older sibling, this Saturday afternoon free time was made available to parents to encourage Christmas shopping. In 1966, kids saw the 1959 Mexican-made kiddie movie *Santa Claus* at Summit Mall. The same low-budget holiday film was also playing at the nearby State Road Shopping Center. The Italian-made 1966 flick *The Christmas That Almost Wasn't* played at Summit Mall. Across town, several Disney movies played throughout the city at several theaters. More and more, the malls and plazas with movie screens scheduled children's holiday features and encouraged parents to shop nearby during the screening. And in 1968, Forest City in Chapel Hill Mall sponsored kiddie matinees at the mall's movie theater throughout the holiday season, encouraging parents with the promise "We'll entertain your kids while you shop." During the month-long 1968 holiday season, children could be dropped off at the theater complex to see Laurel & Hardy and Three Stooges shorts, animal movies such as *Gentle Giant* and *Dog of Flanders Fox,* and the 1966 holiday film *The Christmas That Almost Wasn't.* By offering multiple films in a rotating schedule, it seems apparent that Forest City was hoping that the free babysitting would lure parents to shop in their store more than just once—and potentially several times over the course of the holiday shopping season. It is worth noting how competitive stores became as more and more entertainment was offered in the hopes that it would attract parents to do their shopping at a particular location.

Downtown Akron also hoped to attract shoppers with entertainment for their children. In 1979, O'Neil's sponsored kiddie matinees at the Civic Theatre each Sunday in December, reminding parents to drop off their children while they shopped at

O'Neil's down the street. Charging $1.50 per ticket, children saw family entertainment such as *The Shoemaker and the Elves, The Daydreamer* (the story of Hans Christian Andersen), *Jack and the Beanstalk*, and *March of the Wooden Soldiers*. Event organizers also promised Rudolph would be in the lobby each week with a gift for each child in attendance. For several years in the early 1980s, O'Neil's hosted Kids Korner where children were engaged with holiday crafts while their parents shopped in the store.

ARCHIE RETURNS
A SOCIAL NETWORKING SUCCESS STORY

Archie the Talking Snowman's reign at the mall came to end after the 2003 holiday season. In early 2004, Chapel Hill Mall was sold to new owners, CBL & Associates Properties Inc. from Tennessee, who owned and operated sixty other malls around the country. With diminished attendance and out-of-state owners who weren't familiar with Archie's legacy, the giant snowman was retired. This was an end of an era for Archie and for Akron's Christmas attractions.

As the owners of similar properties throughout the country, CBL had a reputation for acquiring leading malls in middle markets. *Akron Beacon Journal* reporter Mary Etheridge wrote "A company in negotiations to buy Akron's Chapel Hill Mall has a reputation for putting millions of dollars into its shopping centers, drawing first-class tenants and paying close attention to details." But it was the dismissal of one of these "details" that would first gather the attention of another *Beacon Journal* staffer, David Giffels. Late in October 2004, Giffels wrote a column about how the Akron holiday icon, Archie the Snowman was absent from the mall. The new owners of the mall were hosting Santa Claus and other holiday events for the upcoming 2004 holiday season but Archie was no more. "After careful review, it has been decided that Archie will retire this year," said Chapel Hill spokeswoman Andrea Ferraro—quoted in Giffels' column. In recognition of Archie's value to the community, Giffels suggested that Archie be donated to an organization that could showcase the two story holiday icon. "Wouldn't he look great under a pavilion at Akron's Lock 3 park?" He wrote, "Take your kids downtown to see the resurrected O'Neil's window displays, then end the walk with an old, familiar conversation. It just seems a shame to leave the big lug out in the cold." A shame indeed.

Less than two weeks later in 2004, Giffels wrote a follow-up in the newspaper. Chapel Hill Mall had not changed its position about returning Archie to his home but they hadn't yet dismissed all possibilities of donating Archie to someone else. Another spokesperson for the mall's new owners added that Archie was "in a serious state of disrepair" suggesting that if anyone was interested in saving Archie they'd need to rebuild him which would also mean financial backing. The challenges were becoming increasingly high as any future for Archie required the public space to display the twenty-foot snowman and a sizable budget to afford a complete restoration.

Giffels also reported in 2004 that he heard from some passionate Archie fans who were sad about Archie's retirement. Keep in mind that it was adults who responded to the newspaper article—many of whom had made it a tradition over the decades to visit Archie and had counted on bringing their own children and grandchildren to speak with him. Giffels solicited more responses from readers asking for ideas about how to save Archie. However it would be several years before Archie fans would mobilize.

In 2008, the popular blogger Erick Bognar from *Wonderful Wonderblog* wrote an influential post about his nostalgia for Archie the Snowman. Bognar is a specialty writer and toy collector, posting about sci-fi geekiness, monster and horror films, and nerdy pop culture collectibles—he also frequently comments on Christmas culture. Although his blog reaches a national audience, Bognar is a life-long resident of Akron and grew up visiting Archie at Chapel Hill Mall. In December 2008, Bognar posted about Archie, sharing his nostalgic childhood memories about visiting the talking giant, and about taking his son to speak with Archie. Posting a few photos of the mall he found online, Bognar also asked if any of his readers remembered Archie and had any photos. His readers scoured the internet for photos of Akron's Archie and someone even described another talking Christmas attraction from another part of the country. (Sorry Anonymous, but the talking tree at a mall in Indiana seems like nothing compared to Archie. At one time, Akron even featured *two* talking Christmas trees!)

Another of *Wonderful Wonderblog's* readers pointed out Giffels' newspaper columns from 2004 about Archie's retirement. Other readers suggested numerous Facebook discussion groups created for fans of Archie the Snowman to share their memories and post photos on-line. It certainly looked like an awful lot of people were already missing Archie and an increasingly popular social networking platform was helping people gather online in one place and voice their sense of loss over Akron's discontinued holiday traditions.

One of the readers that commented on *Wonderful Wonderblog's* Archie post was a writer for *Cleveland Scene* magazine. Award-winning journalist D. X. Ferris was inspired by Bognar's remembrances to write his own sassy piece for *Scene* in 2008 about Archie's whereabouts. Noting that Archie hadn't been publicly displayed since 2003, Ferris followed up with Chapel Hill Mall in 2008 inquiring about Archie's status. Fearing he was no longer in storage somewhere, Ferris acknowledged that Archie might have already been sent to "a scrap heap." When he got no response for his inquiry from a mall spokesperson encouraged readers to use their own imaginations to visualize Archie's current state in 2008. The conversations both public and private about the talking snowman grew in number in the years during Archie's absence. It took nothing short of a social movement to change Archie's future.

Although journalists, bloggers, and writers were calling for Akron residents to speak up about the loss of everyone's favorite holiday icon, it was someone else entirely who brought people to action. Archie fan extraordinaire, barber/stylist Tommy Uplinger from East Akron eventually found himself in an unexpected role in 2011. Tommy grew up in Akron visiting Archie at the mall when he was a child, and then as a teenager he spent long hours hanging out at the mall. As an adult, Tommy married and found work in another state, moving from his hometown to live in Florida for a number of years. As he tells it, Tommy moved back to Akron in late 2011 and re-connected with friends from his high school years at a bonfire. The conversation eventually turned to the changes in Akron over recent years. Tommy was crushed to hear that Archie the Talking Snowman had been removed from the mall—he had been hoping to bring his toddler son to visit with Archie, an important Christmas experience from his own childhood. In Tommy's own recollections, he claims to have gone online the night of the bonfire to search for photos and other people's memories of Archie. Although several other discussion groups about Archie had already been created, Tommy started his own Facebook group on November 13, 2011 entitled "Bring Archie Back to Chapel Hill Mall." Tommy wondered if other Akronites shared his passion for discussing the possibility of resurrecting the lost tradition.

The response to Tommy's Facebook group was immediate and overwhelming. Within two days, the group had 2,500 members! Tommy asked his friend David Burkett and many others to join him as administrators in the group to help approve all the requests for new members. The earliest discussions in that group included questions about why Chapel Hill Mall had abandoned Archie, where Archie was physically located at that moment, and what could be done to bring Archie back. As the group acquired more and more members, word within the social networking site began to spread and thousands—yes, thousands of people were joining the group within its first few weeks, in November 2011. Tommy, David Burkett and the other administrators were kept busy around the clock accepting new members into the group. At that time, Facebook groups required someone to physically click a button and approve membership for access into groups. Spammers also noticed the group's exploding membership and the admins for Bring Archie Back to Chapel Hill Mall were overwhelmed with adding new members and kicking out spammers trying to sell sunglasses and hawking discount shoe offers.

At the same time, Tommy and his friends were trying to join the ongoing conversations about Archie. No one really knew where Archie was stored, and few had any idea why the mall had stopped displaying Archie. For some new members, the group was the first news that Archie hadn't been at the mall since 2003. What everyone in the group shared in common was a strong memory of the talking snowman and a passion for changing the state of things. People began sharing their childhood memories with Archie, descriptions of Archie's importance to their holiday celebrations, and concern for the next generation of Akron's children's access (or lack thereof) to a cherished holiday tradition. People who had moved away from Akron over the years also found the group, expanding its reach far beyond Akron residents. Hard-to-find photos began surfacing as family after family began uploading old snapshots of children standing in front of the twenty-foot icon. Photos from the thirty-six years of Archie's life began to circulate on Facebook, and even wider onto the world wide web, most often becoming detached from their original owners.

People began making suggestions for Archie's new home. While some of the ideas were thoughtful, others were unrealistic, and a few were best read as punchlines. Some group members thought the only true place for Archie's return should be his original home, Chapel Hill Mall. Others suggested Summit Mall, downtown at the John S. Knight Center during the Holiday Tree Festival, Lock 3, and the Riverfront Mall area in Cuyahoga Falls. Other less helpful suggestions included Rolling Acres (which was already closed by then) or even on top of former TV evangelist Rex Humbard's five-hundred-foot cement tower in Cuyahoga Falls. Tommy remembers commenting that he was even willing to display Archie in his front yard in a desperate effort to do whatever it took to bring the snowman back to Akron's children.

The Facebook group's membership soared and by the fourth day, there were over five thousand members. By the fifth day, there were six thousand members. The admins were overwhelmed with approving more members as well as moderating the discussions. The members of the online group found themselves overwhelmed as well. In those earlier days of Facebook, each time a new user requested membership, a notification was sent to the entire membership. So not only were Tommy, David and all the admins finding that they were inundated with approval requests—so was each of the thousands of new members of the group! People began flooding the Bring Archie Back to Chapel Hill Mall group wall with frustrations about notifications as well as requests for instructions on how to leave the group. As thousands of people were being added, hundreds of those same people were fleeing the group to escape the overwhelming and annoying notifications. Despite members exiting the group, the membership kept increasing and within a few weeks, the group had over ten thousand members. If internet shopping had changed consumer habits and brought an end to Christmas attractions such as Archie the Snowman, perhaps online social media could revive the Christmas traditions we missed.

People felt the powerful energy of the online discussions about Archie and they wanted to do something about what they felt was the tragic error of Archie's retirement. With that amount of traffic in one Facebook group, you can also imagine the headaches. Not everyone was serious about recalling their treasured memories of Akron's Christmas icon. At times peoples' jokes became vulgar and a volley of comments would be lobbed to silence another. In an attempt to be professional and respectful, Tommy requested information from the mall about Archie's whereabouts and the possibility of his return. Soon, people began posting in the Facebook group that they too had telephoned the mall, emailed the mall, and some even claimed they showed up in person at the information service desk to demand answers to their questions. It's no wonder that the inundated Chapel Hill Mall didn't respond to requests for information about Archie in those first few weeks. Tommy and David pleaded with members of the group to allow them to speak for everyone. Control over the popular movement would take calm heads and a business-like approach.

By Thanksgiving 2011, Tommy and his friend David knew that thousands of people were hoping to find a way to have Archie the Snowman return for Akron's children. Unaware that in years past, the mall required a month's time to install Archie and that Archie was typically open before Thanksgiving, Tommy and David worked feverishly to see if their popular movement could bring Archie back to the mall for the 2011 Christmas season. They began sending out press releases, hoping that someone with more power and influence could help communicate with Chapel Hill Mall and get some results.

Four days after Thanksgiving in 2011, Tommy created a new Facebook page for fans to follow, The Bring Back Archie the Snowman page. He asked everyone in the group to "like" the Facebook fan page and many thousands did just that. Overwhelmed with the requirement to approve all new members into the group, the new page allowed Facebookers to avoid spammers entirely, and admins could control what was being said (no more vulgar language and mean-spirited posts) more effectively. New followers to the page only needed to add themselves and followers could better control how many updates they wanted to receive. A social networking success story was underway.

What happened next surprised everyone involved. During the first week of December 2011, the press releases about the history of Archie the Talking Snowman, his retirement, and the Facebook group of thousands of members, went viral. Not only did the local journalists pick up the story but the Associated Press circulated the odd tale about a twenty-foot snowman. The story was carried in papers and online news sources around the country. It was picked up by news sources on both the East and West coasts and throughout the Midwest. Soon, Tommy and David were asked to speak on two local radio interviews—Akron's WAKR and WNIR talk radio. Then the men circulated the audio clips of the radio shows throughout Facebook.

Cleveland TV stations also brought their cameras and Uplinger, Burkett, and a few others found themselves explaining how important Archie was to Akronites. An investigative TV reporter with WOIO Channel 19 from Cleveland convinced an employee from Chapel Hill to speak on camera. It was during this interview that most people heard for the first time that Archie no longer existed—he had been disassembled and placed in trash dumpsters years before.

Although this was sad news and Archie fans expressed their disappointment online, it wasn't surprising news to others. Tommy and David didn't give up on their goal when they heard that Archie was destroyed. Instead, their efforts took a different tack. Soon discussions on Facebook were dominated by efforts to fundraise in order to build a new Archie! The next step forward required the identification of an organization with a suitable public location. Throughout December 2011, Uplinger and his growing crew of helpers continued to raise awareness about Archie.

Uplinger and Burkett quickly organized a Ride Along event to gather people to help spread the word about bringing Archie back. The Ride Along event was organized to unite interested people on a drive through Akron, to honk their car horns, share their passion, and raise awareness for Archie the Snowman. On December 11th, 2011, the Ride Along event began in an empty parking lot across the street from Chapel Hill Mall and involved 25–30 vehicles. Many of the automobiles bore specially made Bring Back Archie decals in their windows. And others made poster board signs to wave and show off their message and support for Archie. This was the first time the organizers and many in the newly formed social media group met face-to-face. The group of cars left the Chapel Hill Mall, traveled down Howe Avenue to downtown Akron and Lock 3, and circled back to Chapel Hill.

The Ride Along event was also the day that Ra'ul Umaña stepped forward and introduced himself to Uplinger and Burkett. Although Christmas was just two short weeks away, Uplinger, Burkett and Umaña agreed to continue working on bringing back Archie with the new goal of the Christmas season the following year, in 2012.

Happy memories of Archie inspired artistic expression. Candie Ujhazy wrote a poem about Archie the Snowman in December 2011 to express how much she missed him.

"Archie the Snowman"
 by Candie Ujhazy

Archie is the name;
I didn't want to go.
I did not melt;
I wasn't made with real snow.

Kids came to visit me;
Each and every year.
Some moved away;
Then came back to here.

Not only to find;
That I was gone.
But, many would have been happy;
To put me on their snow covered lawn.

My home was sold;
They threw me in the trash.
Little did they know;
The mall, people would bash.

I don't think that they expected;
The things that they did hear.
"We want ARCHIE back;"
And "We want him this year."

Many people came together;
On a Facebook page.
And the "mall lady;"
Slammed the door with rage.

The news and media;
All pitched in.
Asking about Archie;

Got them no grin.

"He is gone;"
Is what they said.
They threw me away;
Didn't just put me to bed.

Drove around town;
Making people aware.
That I was gone;
And was wanted back there.

They do not want me;
At the mall.
They do not want me;
Not at all.

To find a new home;
Is the key.
Perhaps in downtown Akron;
At awesome Lock 3.

Things are still;
In the works.
Must work out the details;
And a few quirks.

Archie was an icon;
Just so you know.
He WILL return one day;
And to see him, we and our children, will go.

During the first week of January 2012, Uplinger announced on Facebook that he had received an email from the city of Akron's Deputy Mayor David Lieberth to schedule a meeting to discuss the future of Archie. Uplinger also heard from representatives in the city of Cuyahoga Falls interested in hosting Archie at the Riverfront area if the city of Akron wasn't committed. The first meeting was scheduled in February 2012. Tommy's goal was to find a permanent home for Archie and not just a quick solution for one year. It would be months before Uplinger and Burkett heard back about whether the city of Akron was on board.

By the end of summer 2012, it was officially announced that the city of Akron was committed to bringing Archie back for Akron's children. It was Lieberth who had forwarded the development of Lock 3 and championed its many uses over the years. It was fortuitous that Lieberth saw that Archie would be a wonderful complement to Lock 3's annual holiday festivities. It was also Lieberth's efforts that acquired the corporate sponsorship necessary to fund the rebuilding of Archie.

Since Archie's return meant they were starting from scratch, Lieberth asked Uplinger and Burkett if they knew someone to help build the new snowman. From the start, the former Chapel Hill Mall employee and longtime Archie supporter Ra'ul Umaña was offered the contract to create the new snowman. In one of his last projects before retirement in September 2012, Lieberth gave Umaña the okay to move forward to rebuild Archie. However, the clock was ticking. The all-new Archie needed to be open to the public by Thanksgiving and there were only a few short months to rebuild the larger-than-life snowman for all to see.

Ra'ul began assembling artist friends and volunteers to help him reconstruct Archie and design and install Archie's Enchanted Encounter at Lock 3 in the basement space beneath the former O'Neil's department store building. The importance and historical significance of the new location for Archie's home should not be overlooked. The Rubber City's Christmas cultural heritage was coming alive again, in of all places, the repurposed O'Neil's store basement.

Volunteers stepped forward to help in the cause. Local artists, civic-minded community builders, Archie fans, and families gathered together to pitch in and work. Some volunteers worked for an afternoon while others devoted dozens of hours of their

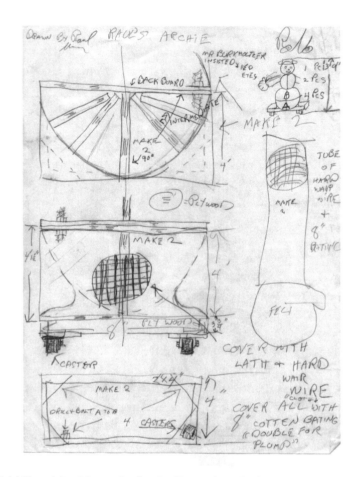

Ra'ul Umaña's hand drawn plan for rebuilding Archie at Lock 3 in 2012.

time—all working to create a holiday experience for our city's youngsters and to recreate some of the wonder and spectacle of Akron's Christmases past. The mission was to create the largest, most awe-inspiring display possible in the hope of providing a richer, more heartfelt experience for everyone. The volunteers worked as a team to get done whatever tasked needed to be completed each day.

Archie's Enchanted Encounter not only included a newly built Archie the Talking Snowman but also incorporated displays of mechanical figures of favorite children's storybook characters from the former O'Neil's display collection. After Lawrence and Cynthia Nixon selected the two animatronic sets they put on display annually in the Polsky's building corner windows, the staff at Lock 3 gave Umaña and the volunteers permission to use the rest of the former O'Neil's display collection.

Umaña designed the Archie Encounter to include a walking path from display to display. He imagined the path to resemble the sidewalk and visitors walking from window to window, as if once again walking along Main Street gazing into O'Neil's many sections of window displays. Even the spaces in between the display windows were built and painted to resemble the exterior of O'Neil's store! As visitors looked into each display "window," they laid their eyes upon vintage O'Neil's mechanical figures set up in their former glory—minus the window panes. Also used in the 2012 Archie's Enchanted Encounter were giant Nutcracker figures gifted to Lock 3 by the German visitors from the Christkindle Market. There was also a collection of gingerbread themed items (dolls, cookie jars, and more) on loan from a private collector.

I asked Jason Pullin of Akron in an email interview about why he got involved as a volunteer with the re-installation of Archie at Lock 3. "I really wanted to help with the project because I am the father of two children," he said. "When I was a kid I remember going to see Archie every year and even as an adult. It's important to have things like this to be able to spend quality time with family around the holidays." Pullin was one of more than three dozen people who worked to restore one of Akron's favorite Christmas traditions.

In building Archie at Lock 3, Umaña followed the same design plan he had first used at Chapel Hill Mall almost three decades earlier. The two bottom portions of Archie were built from wood in sections, much like the segmented body of an orange or grapefruit. The wood was then covered in chicken wire and wrapped in layers of white, cottony batten. The little house which hides the person supplying the voice of Archie was placed amongst the many decorations in the display which surrounded the giant snowman.

Archie installed at Lock 3 in 2012. Photo: Shane Wynn.

THE STORY OF ARCHIE THE TALKING SNOWMAN

There were a couple changes made to the snowman—alterations from his days at Chapel Hill Mall. One change was his height. Knowing that children are most often struck by Archie's immense size, the goal was to keep Archie as large as possible. However, the ceiling height in the basement of the former O'Neil's building was lower than the two story ceiling at the mall. Umaña built the new Archie to reach all the way to the rafters at Lock 3—which made him fifteen feet tall, a little bit shorter than the previous twenty feet tall. To allow Archie to stand at maximum height, his former signature top hat was replaced with a more form-fitting ball cap. Most people were pleased to see that Archie's height was still high enough to be breathtaking to small children. Another alteration Umaña made was to change Archie's eye color to a softer, gentler blue, in contrast to the original glaring red eyes of years past. Umaña also changed the lights in Archie's eyes from standard bulbs to more modern, efficient LED lights.

The elaborate complexity of cleaning the aging mechanical display items, restoring and reclothing figures, and repairing motors to working order, as well as building Archie from scratch—all by the Thanksgiving deadline—was a nearly impossible task. Running out of time, Lock 3 hired additional help to finish what Umaña and the team weren't able to complete.

On the day after Thanksgiving, Friday, November 23, 2012, Archie the Talking Snowman made his debut at the annual Holiday Lighting Ceremony. Joining Mayor Plusquellic at the gala event was Mrs. Buchholzer (the widow of Richard Buchholzer, the original developer/owner of Chapel Hill Mall and Archie the Snowman), Deputy Mayor David Lieberth, Ra'ul Umaña, Tommy Uplinger, David Burkett, and thousands of Akron residents. After speeches of congratulations and crediting all those involved, local singer/songwriter Hal Walker performed an original song about Archie the Snowman. The event concluded with fireworks. Archie the Snowman was back!

Visitors to Archie's Enchanted Encounter enjoyed many other wintry activities available at Lock 3 Park's Holidayfest including ice skating, the toboggan run, boutique shopping at the Christkindle

Market wooden booths, and the various other activities organized by Lock 3. Holidayfest activities and events were made possible by the financial support of local organizations and businesses. In 2012, Archie the Snowman was sponsored by Chapel Hill Mall and no tax dollars were used for Archie's return.

Over the 2012 holiday season, thousands of people visited Lock 3 to interact with Archie. Many walked the zigzag path through the former O'Neil's animatronic storybook character displays, across the newly built wooden platform to speak with Archie to share their Christmas wishes, and to get their photo taken with the frozen giant.

In 2012, there was even a photo contest held to connect Facebook followers with the newly built Archie. Cuyahoga Falls resident Ronda Roxbury and her children won the photo contest and they received free Archie t-shirts. Roxbury shared with me that she and her husband both grew up visiting Archie each year when they were children. She said,

> "We were so crushed when Archie was removed from the mall. When I saw on Facebook that Tommy Uplinger and David Burkett started a drive to bring Archie back, I was all over that…I was excited to see that so many people were so excited to bring back a piece of their family's traditions and to start a new [Archie.]…My boys still wear their Archie t-shirts…as do I. Making memories, that is what Archie is all about."

Archie's Enchanted Encounter at Lock 3 was so hugely successful that the attraction was repeated the following year. However, Archie and the former O'Neil's animated figures collection needed a new custodian. Jeanne Jordan, a seasonal display designer with more than ten years experience, was hired to design and set up the Archie Encounter for the 2013 holiday season. Jordan grew up in Akron's North Hill and fondly remembered the wonderment of the fantasy window displays at Polsky's and O'Neil's from her youth. Her childhood experiences inspired her to pursue a career as a window designer as an adult. In the basement of the former O'Neil's building, Jordan added lower barriers to the display spaces

The Roxbury family's winning photo from the 2012 Archie Facebook photo contest.

so children could better see each exhibition but not be able to touch the delicate vintage figures. To prepare for the 2013 holiday season, Jordan didn't need to reassemble Archie—he stayed right where he was built and was covered to keep him clean and dry. However, the former O'Neil's mechanical figures and the window displays had to be taken down each year, and placed in storage to protect and preserve them. For the 2013 holiday season, Archie's second year at Lock 3, Jordan redesigned and installed each display space with the moving storybook characters from the original O'Neil's store collection. Lawrence and Cynthia Nixon also used two of

Archie the Snowman on display at Chapel Hill Mall in 2014. Photo: Dominic Caruso.

the sets from the same collection to decorate the corner windows in the Polsky's building on Main Street. Downtown Akron had not seen this much holiday spirit for decades. Akron residents flocked to stand in awe of the Christmas displays for another year. Now in its second year, visiting Lock 3's Archie the Talking Snowman and the former O'Neil's animated displays was becoming a tradition once again.

A financial crisis in the summer of 2014 brought a new wrinkle and unexpected changes. Like many malls across the country, Chapel Hill was struggling financially due to changing consumer habits and a loss of customers. In the summer of 2014, when the mall owners defaulted on loans, Chapel Hill fell into foreclosure. A Summit County judge appointed an experienced management company, McKinley Inc. as receivers to keep the retail facility open for business. No one in Akron wanted to see a second disaster, one such as Rolling Acres on the city's west side—an abandoned mall whose roof had collapsed. Photographs from break-ins at Rolling Acres captured national attention as examples of failures of mall culture. Although Rolling Acres was first developed and owned by the team of Richard Buchholzer and Forest City Enterprises—as was Chapel Hill Mall—both malls had been sold several times and had different owners. The blight of Rolling Acres had been exacerbated by bankruptcy and legal issues of ownership—and continues to this day. However, quick action was taken in the financial troubles of Chapel Hill Mall to avoid a second mall closing.

The new Chapel Hill Mall management team in 2014 was looking for a way to bring shoppers back to the mall during the holidays. Working closely with city officials, the popular Archie the Snowman was moved by truck from Lock 3 to the center court in Chapel Hill Mall. On Saturday, November 22, 2014, Chapel Hill Mall debuted the return of Archie the Talking Snowman—his first time back at the mall in ten years, since the holiday season of 2003.

Hundreds of people turned up for the big unveiling. Among those in the crowd stood Ra'ul Umaña, the former Chapel Hill Mall employee who had worked as the voice of Archie, helped

Ra'ul Umaña (dressed as Father Christmas) and Tommy Uplinger pause to take a selfie near the Archie display at Chapel Hill Mall in 2014. Photo: Dominic Caruso.

to install Archie for many years at the mall, and who had been responsible for rebuilding Archie at Lock 3. Also in the crowd was Tommy Uplinger, the man who had launched the successful social networking movement to bring Archie back to our city's youngsters. Tommy and his son Liam were the first people Archie spoke to on that Saturday morning at the premiere event. Unfortunately, Tommy's friend David Burkett, who worked along side him to rally the popular movement on behalf of Archie, was not at the mall event. Burkett had died unexpectedly in the spring of 2014 and his absence made the unveiling bittersweet for many. Ra'ul Umaña, who appeared frail at the November debut of Archie, passed on just a few months later, after a long struggle with cancer, in January 2015. The appeal of speaking with Akron celebrity, Archie the Snowman drew in the crowds at Chapel Hill during the holiday shopping season. Can Archie help to save the mall that first gave him life? We'll have to wait and see.

Akron's Christmas cultural heritage continues today in many parts of the city both in spirit and in actual historical display pieces.

Joanna Wilson, Ra'ul Umaña, and Tommy Uplinger near the Archie display at Chapel Hill Mall in 2014. Photo: Dominic Caruso.

As of the holiday season in 2014, the following local Christmas attractions are what Akron residents can still enjoy. The former O'Neil's department store mechanical figures of favorite children's storybook characters were on display at Lock 3 during the holiday season in 2014. Although Archie the Snowman was removed from that space and put on display at Chapel Hill Mall, the animatronic figures continued to delight. Many people still don't know that these original O'Neil's display sets still exist and have been exhibited downtown for the past twenty-five years. In Archie's absence, the staff at Lock 3 added the family activity of putt-putt golf in the space adjacent to the displays of the animated figures. While the attempt to incorporate a family-friendly activity was laudable, the inclusion of a putt-putt course didn't seem to fit the spirit of the classic displays.

Jeanne Jordan, the seasonal display designer working at Lock 3, expressed that she would like to see the city and community invest in restoring the collection of animatronic figures. The figures must be packed away after each holiday season, however the storage

Peter Pan animatronic display installed at Lock 3 in 2014. Photo: Dominic Caruso.

space set aside for them is moist and dirty. Each figure's motor runs the entire holiday season and therefore they wear down, necessitating constant repairs and upkeep for all the figures. Replacing the figures is nearly impossible and what isn't restored and preserved today will soon be gone forever. Jordan even suggests the city expand their collection of Christmas display pieces to enhance the current collection. Other cities have purchased vintage display sets and draw in visitors from out of town to see them. Why couldn't Akron do it too?

As of Christmas 2014, the corner windows of the Polsky's building—now owned by the University of Akron—were decorated with two animatronic sets from the original O'Neil's collection as well. When I last spoke with Lawrence and Cynthia Nixon, the experienced team that have lovingly looked after the entire collection since 1997, they said they were looking to retire from designing the Polsky's window displays. Jeanne Jordan, who has been working at Lock 3 to exhibit the rest of the O'Neil's collection, has expressed interest in continuing the Polsky's building

Brenda Fargo's Journey to Bethlehem display (2014) in the windows of the Mayflower Manor in downtown Akron, Ohio. Photo: Dominic Caruso.

displays. It is hoped that the downtown tradition will continue in years to come.

In 2014, residents also enjoyed the finely detailed Journey to Bethlehem miniatures display in the Mayflower Manor's windows along Main Street next to the Polsky's building. Akron resident Brenda Fargo grew up mesmerized by the annual Christmas window displays put out by O'Neil's and Polsky's of decades past. Fargo has collected and personally owns the 1000+ piece collection of miniatures she uses to design and construct the Journey to Bethlehem display each year. What started off as a display she enjoyed installing at her church has grown to become a much larger exhibition for the public. Her display is an attempt at an authentic depiction of Bethlehem at the time of Christ's birth. She's been filling the downtown Mayflower Manor windows with her sacred exhibit since 2004.

The miniatures are manufactured by Fontanini, made of hand-painted plastic and resin. Other miniatures in the collection are made by Fargo herself. She redesigns and adds to the display each

The Nativity scene in Brenda Fargo's *Journey to Bethlehem* (2014) display at the Mayflower Manor in downtown Akron, Ohio. Photo: Dominic Caruso.

year to keep it fresh for the viewers that return year after year, and to use more pieces from her immense collection. Adding interest to the expansive display, Fargo creates a new "Find It List" each year. The lists are suggestions for what to locate hidden in plain sight within the complex and vast assemblage, such as specific water fowl, a grouping of angels, or a shopkeeper wearing a funny hat. Fargo hopes the "Find It Lists" provide a reason for viewers to linger in front of the windows and interact with the display more. She's also overheard families create contests amongst themselves to determine who can find the list items first. Although it takes months of her free time to assemble the display each year, and months to pack it away again, she loves doing it. It not only

O'Neil's life-size Nativity set on display in 2014 at the Cornerstone Church, at Portage Lakes. Photo: Dominic Caruso.

creates a reason for Akronites to come back downtown and enjoy Christmas window displays again but the Bethlehem display also shares her sense of reverence for the holiday season.

At Christmas time, in 2014, Akron residents also saw the former O'Neil's store life-size Nativity display exhibited in the front of Cornerstone Church, a Free Methodist Church at Portage Lakes, just south of the city. Hundreds of people each year gather after the Wednesday evening, Thanksgiving Eve church service for the display's unveiling. The Nativity display is the same one that was first used by O'Neil's in 1955, and which stood atop the department store's marquee for two decades. The Nativity display was purchased by Cornerstone Church in the 1980s and the congregation has been good stewards of its care. The twenty-three piece, life-size, all white, hollow figures are made from what appears to be fiberglass construction. When needed, the figures have been restored using foam repair materials. Although vandals destroyed the baby Jesus figure and a goat disintegrated several years back, the rest of the set is in remarkably good shape considering its age.

If you haven't seen this amazing Nativity display recently, you are overlooking an awe-inspiring piece of Akron Christmas history.

What does the future hold for Archie the Talking Snowman and Akron's Christmas cultural heritage? This big question shouldn't be limited to a response about bringing shopping back downtown. Polsky's closed in 1978 and O'Neil's in 1989. Despite this, downtown storefront windows have been decorated nearly every year for the past fifteen years. After Archie's retirement in the early 2000s, the city witnessed the power of its residents coming together to bring Archie back, a Christmas tradition that was sorely missed. While Chapel Hill Mall's future is uncertain, Archie has been promised to return to Lock 3 if need be. What are we willing to do to make sure that what we have now isn't lost again? Did you bring your children or grandchildren to speak with Archie at the mall in 2014?

Another big question is how much do we value our city's Christmas cultural heritage? To be honest, most residents I've spoken with have no idea that the mechanical figures on display downtown are former O'Neil's store display items. Some others don't even care. If you didn't grow up in Akron and didn't experience the joy of these Christmas window displays, can we expect you to care? As our population continues to age and those that remember the glory of Akron's Christmas culture pass away, what will sustain the future of these items? Can the twenty-first century's children brought up with video games and electronic devices appreciate the simple wonder of gently moving mechanical figures in storybook displays? Or a live conversation with a giant talking snowman? When I witness a child looking with wonder at Archie in Chapel Hill, or a young family gazing into the Polsky's building windows at the Wizard of Oz animatronic figures, I believe the younger generation of Akronites can appreciate Akron's Christmas culture. But it's up to all of us to be good stewards of the Christmas treasures we have from our city's past.

Photo: Chris Rutan Photography

THE STORY OF ARCHIE THE TALKING SNOWMAN

ABOUT JOANNA WILSON

Joanna Wilson is an author who specializes in writing about Christmas entertainment, most notably *Tis the Season TV: the Encyclopedia of Christmas-Themed Episodes, Specials, and Made-for-TV Movies* (2010). In 2010 she appeared as a commentator in *The Real Story of Christmas* on the History Channel, and the TV Guide Network's *25 Most Hilarious Holiday TV Moments*. Wilson writes a prominent blog about Christmas on TV at www. ChristmasTVHistory.com.

Additionally, Wilson is the author of local history / nostalgia books, including *A is for Akron: an A to Z List of Akron's Places and Things that Make Us Smile* with Karen Starr (2014), and *The Story of Archie* (2015). She is the co-founder and co-writer of the popular blog *Akron Empire,* and she is a regular columnist for the newspaper *The Devil Strip.* Joanna counts herself as one of Highland Square's many memorable characters.

ALSO FROM AUTHOR JOANNA WILSON
& 1701 PRESS

❄ Merry Musical Christmas ❄
Volume One
The Best Christmas Music in TV Sitcoms & Dramas

Merry Musical Christmas, Volume One is the first in a five-volume series featuring the best Christmas Music from television history. Focusing on the best holiday music in Sitcoms & Dramas, this volume contains inspiring, outstanding, and surprising performances by some of television's brightest stars, from their roles on classic shows as well as sleepers, and from early sitcoms like The *Adventures of Ozzie and Harriet* to important contemporary hits like *Glee.*

**Available at www.ChristmasTVHistory.com
& Amazon.com**

ALSO FROM AUTHOR JOANNA WILSON & 1701 PRESS

the Christmas TV Companion

a Guide to Cult Classics, Strange Specials & Outrageous Oddities

Christmas on TV is wilder, weirder, & more wondrous than you think! *The Christmas TV Companion* is a funny, engaging look beyond the same Christmas specials that air every year to the cult TV rarities, over-the-top made-for-TV holiday specials, & bizarre, spacey shows that truly expand the notion of "Christmas spirit." Loaded with pop culture references, this book is sure to please pop aficionados & TV junkies of all stripes. Its remarkable breadth of content covers the far-out gems of yesterday, as well as the irreverent & cutting edge Christmas material of today, from Arthur C. Clarke to *South Park,* and from Ed Sullivan to *Squidbillies.* This guide also contains practical examples for enhancing your own Christmas TV viewing.

Available at www.ChristmasTVHistory.com & Amazon.com

If you enjoyed *The Story of Archie the Talking Snowman,* please post a review of the book to Amazon.com, Goodreads, or your favorite online site to share books. Your reviews help us to spread the word about this book.